One Life

Hope, Healing and Inspiration on the Path to Recovery from Eating Disorders

Naomi Feigenbaum

Foreword by Gayle Brooks, Ph.D.

Jessica Kingsley Publishers
London and Philadelphia

First published in 2009
by Jessica Kingsley Publishers
116 Pentonville Road
London N1 9JB, UK
and
400 Market Street, Suite 400
Philadelphia, PA 19106, USA

www.jkp.com

Copyright © Naomi Feigenbaum 2009
Foreword copyright © Gayle Brooks 2009

Library of Congress Cataloging in Publication Data
A CIP catalog record for this book is available from the Library of Congress

British Library Cataloguing in Publication Data
A CIP catalogue record for this book is available from the British Library

ISBN 978 1 84310 912 9

Printed and bound in Great Britain by
Athenaeum Press, Gateshead, Tyne and Wear

One Life

Books are to be returned on or before
the last date below.

05 JAN 2016		

www.librex.co.uk

of related interest

Beating Eating Disorders Step by Step
A Self-Help Guide for Recovery
Anna Paterson
ISBN 978 1 84310 340 0

Inside Anorexia
The Experiences of Girls and their Families
Christine Halse, Anne Honey and Desiree Boughtwood
ISBN 978 1 84310 597 8

Bulimics on Bulimia
Edited by Maria Stavrou
ISBN 978 1 84310 668 5

Anorexics on Anorexia
Edited by Rosemary Shelley
ISBN 978 1 85302 471 9

Dedicated to Bekah and Jodi
with gratitude
You go above and beyond
and truly make a difference.

Author's Note

While this book indicates signs and symptoms of eating disorders and demonstrates healthy coping skills for recovery, it is not meant to take the place of professional guidance or therapy.

The names of the eleven chapters correspond to the eleven weeks I spent in treatment at the Renfrew Center, however the accompanying skills and stories are not meant to indicate that recovery is a simple linear progression. It is not as though skill one is mastered in week one, skill two in week two and so on. The skills are presented in this way to aid in the understanding and mastery of each skill and to demonstrate them practically and clearly.

Names have been changed to protect confidentiality.

Contents

Acknowledgments

I want to thank my family and true friends, who stuck by me through my most challenging times and never gave up hope. Your support is truly appreciated. Thank you to my wonderful parents who, despite your frustrations, remained calm (mostly) and did everything in your power to provide me with the best treatment. Thank you to my siblings, Adina, Lolly (Sarah) and Yoey (Joseph), who acted with such composure and grace throughout my treatment process. Thank you for your continuing support.

Thank you to Rabbi Burnstein for genuinely caring, for visiting me and always making yourself available to talk, listen and answer questions, and for taking the time to fully understand what I was going through and ensuring that I could participate in all aspects of treatment.

Thank you to Alcoa Inc. for your excellent health benefits.

Thank you to everyone who called, wrote and visited me in treatment.

Thank you to everyone who participated in my treatment: my doctors, therapists, nutritionists, and psychiatrists. To Dr. Gillespie for really "getting it" and for your motivating pep-talks. To Lili for your emails and for your support the night before I went to Renfrew. To the nursing staff at the Cleveland Clinic who do so much, and always with a kind word and a smile. To the staff at the Cleveland Center for Eating Disorders (CCED), who do lifesaving work.

I would like to express gratitude to everyone at Renfrew. Thank you to the kitchen staff for accommodating me and taking such care to provide genuinely kosher meals. To Terri for getting kosher ingredients and cookware so that I could participate in the cooking groups, and to Jeannette for including me in the restaurant trips. Thank you to the psych-techs and counselors for your compassion and empathy. To Jodi W. for your patience and persistence. Thank you to nurse Susan for getting me my favorite colors of Powerade and for being so warm and kind. To Kandi for singing in the med-line and to all the nurses for your patience and dedication. Thank you to the red team staff for reading my long letters and notes at team rounds, always listening to and considering what I had to say. To Vivian for your extreme patience and dependability. Thank you to Jay, AKA "Renfrew Dad," for always doing everything you can to make Renfrew welcoming and pleasant. And thank you to Bekah and Jodi for being two of the best role models I have ever known. You inspire me.

Thank you to the wonderful women I have met on my journey of recovery for your support, empathy, and friendship. A special thank you to "Danielle" and "Amelia." I am honored to call you friends.

Thank you to those who encouraged me to write this book, and to those whose names appear within. Thank you to Lily and Jessica Kingsley Publishers for believing in this project and for helping me spread my message of hope.

Foreword

Millions of young women and men around the world are waging a daily life and death battle with eating disorders such as anorexia and bulimia. While far too many will lose that battle this year, many others will find the path to recovery. Naomi's story is an account of one young woman's courageous journey from near death to the discovery of a life worth living.

Eating disorders are serious psychiatric disorders. Anorexia nervosa which has the highest mortality rate of any mental illness is a dangerous condition in which a person literally starves themselves to death. In Western cultures, anorexia typically strikes 1 in 100 young girls in their early teens, however, as the incidence of anorexia is increasing, girls as young as seven and older women in midlife are also falling victim. The incidence among young men is also rising. For every four women with anorexia, there is one male suffering from the disorder. Along with self-starvation, other symptoms of anorexia include distorted body image (viewing oneself as fat even though one is thin), intense, overwhelming fear of fat and weight gain and refusal to increase nutritional intake even though suffering devastating consequences. At its worse, anorexia is characterized by intense denial that one even has a problem.

Bulimia, another equally serious eating disorder is characterized by a pattern of binge eating followed by vomiting, taking laxatives or diuretics, or abuse of exercise to rid the body of food or calories consumed. As with anorexia, there is often times distorted body image and a fear and preoccupation with becoming fat even though weight is normal. The physical and emotional consequences of bulimia can be devastating. Along with tooth decay, ulcers, and pancreatitis, the loss of body fluids from purging can cause severe dehydration, irregular heartbeats, and cardiac arrest. Episodes of bulimia are often accompanied by feeling out of control, followed by feelings of disgust, guilt, and depression. In the United Status and other Western cultures, 4 out of 100 girls will develop bulimia, typically during late adolescence and young adulthood. For every ten girls suffering from bulimia, one male is battling the disorder. Men who are involved in sports or professions with weight requirements such as body building, wrestling, gymnastics, modeling or entertainment are at increased risk of developing bulimia. Similar to anorexia, the incidence of bulimia is steadily increasing and is now more prevalent in diverse ethnic and socio-cultural groups such as Hispanics, African American, Asian and Native Americans.

Eating disorders are about much more than just food and weight. They may start out as an innocent desire to diet in order to lose a few pounds. However, for some vulnerable individuals they can quickly spiral into a life-threatening condition which takes over every aspect of life and destroys any hope for the future. Eating disorders are not about vanity but rather are rooted in deep feelings of insecurity, low self-esteem, self-loathing, and emotional pain. Psychologically, eating-disorder behaviors serve many purposes such as a means of coping with difficult feelings, establishing a sense of identity, avoiding painful traumatic memories, and gaining control over aspects of life which feel out of control.

Treatment for an eating disorder is most effective when a specialized team of practitioners work together to address the psychological, nutritional, and medical aspects of the illness. Many individuals can be treated successfully by a team of professionals on an outpatient basis. However, as in Naomi's case, some young women, due to the severity of their illness, need an intensive, structured treatment environment such as The Renfrew Center. Within the residential setting of Renfrew, young women receive the psychotherapy, medical and nutritional interventions necessary to heal their bodies and minds. Along with learning how to feed and care for themselves again they are supported in confronting their fears of food, feelings, relationships, and life in general. The Renfrew Center provides young women like Naomi an opportunity to join into a therapeutic community of other young women and girls who share similar struggles. Together they experience a level of interpersonal connection, safety and understanding which encourages them to slowly emerge from their self-imposed isolation. Additionally, Renfrew's intensive therapy program which includes individual and family therapy, a wide array of groups, and nonverbal therapies such as art and movement therapy is integral in helping these young women to develop a self-identity based on who they are rather than on how they look.

Through Naomi's journal writings, she offers a rare glimpse into the mental torment which belies the puzzling behavior of self-starvation. Eating-disorder behavior often becomes a language to communicate thoughts, feelings, needs and desires for which words seem either inadequate or too frightening to utter. By sharing her innermost thoughts we come to understand the paradoxical language of Naomi's eating-disorder behaviors. "...I didn't know how to say that I needed more help. So instead I acted out. I restricted, I cut corners in treatment, and I showed everyone how miserable I was." Naomi's account of her trip to hell and back eloquently demonstrates the healing power of therapeutic relationships. She candidly shares how the push, pull, and ultimate embrace of such relationships helped her to grow up, find her voice, and learn to love and appreciate herself.

What is truly remarkable about Naomi's journey towards recovery is that along the way, she has discovered her life's purpose. That purpose is to help others suffering from eating disorders – who better than someone who has truly been there and done that. By sharing the wisdom and insights learned during her treatment experiences, Naomi inspires others to reach out for help and to know that recovery is possible. The unique way that Naomi combines the telling of her story along with the teaching of practical coping skills from her "tool book" creates a wonderful, down-to-earth guide for anyone searching for recovery.

While someone does not choose to have an eating disorder, recovery is in fact a daily, hourly, and sometimes minute by minute series of choices. Naomi takes us through her personal battle with the devastating illness of anorexia and the triumphant choices which propel her along the road to recovery. Naomi is winning the battle but she honestly acknowledges the road to recovery is often bumpy, with many ups and downs, starts and stops. The journey is at times exhausting, confusing, frustrating, and downright terrifying. But the realization that she has this "one life" is the beacon of hope that lights the way.

Gayle Brooks, Ph.D.
Vice President and Clinical Director
Renfrew Center of Florida

Preface

What is an eating disorder?

Many people mistakenly believe that an eating disorder is simply an unhealthy obsession with food and feeling fat. In truth it is much more than that. An eating disorder is a maladaptive coping mechanism. The sufferer may believe that through manipulation of her food intake she is taking charge of a stressful situation and somehow gaining control.

An eating disorder can be a form of self-punishment or a misguided attempt at communication. The underlying message, "look what you did to me" is not altogether uncommon. An eating disorder pleads, "help me!" and simultaneously warns, "back off!"

Anorexia nervosa trapped me in a world of conflicting extremes. I longed for comfort and support, yet I chased away my friends and family. I refused to eat, yet my thoughts were consumed with food. I demanded perfection, yet I saw failure. I felt I was acting strong, yet I was weakened to the verge of death. Torn constantly in so many different directions, I didn't know if or how to get help. All I knew was that I hurt inside. And, somehow, it seemed right that I should hurt outside as well.

An eating disorder is an external sign of an internal struggle.

In order to recover I had to look inside myself and find out what was really going on. I had to accept responsibility for my own life and well-being. I had to acquire new and healthy coping skills. I had to learn new ways to communicate my pain.

At the Renfrew Center, a leading residential treatment facility for women struggling with a wide variety of eating disorders, I learned that I did not choose to have an eating disorder but that I *do* have the ability to choose recovery.

This book is intended to show women and girls who have eating disorders that they themselves are the only ones who can affect change, and to provide hope that, under any circumstances, recovery is possible. It is intended to help friends and family members of these women understand the experience of an eating disorder. This book illustrates the progression of my treatment and recovery and demonstrates that residential treatment is extremely effective in helping women recover from eating disorders. This story also reveals the importance of the therapeutic relationship.

It is common knowledge that one should not attempt to heal from an eating disorder on one's own. Sometimes women are reluctant to enter treatment because they fear the unknown. *One Life* details the inner workings of residential treatment and is thus an invaluable resource for women with eating disorders and their loved ones in making decisions regarding treatment options. Oftentimes there is a great deal of denial and this book can help readers identify traits that may indicate an eating disorder.

Each chapter opens with a positive coping skill that can be utilized by women struggling with eating disorders to help them lead healthier and more fulfilling lives. Throughout the chapter the new skill is demonstrated through my personal experiences. Whereas many books concerning eating disorders are clinical in nature, stressing primarily the symptoms and damage to the body, *One Life* gets to the heart and soul of the experience of having an eating disorder. It focuses on the ways in which one's internal world is shaken and how over time, with treatment, cognitive distortions can be rectified.

I believe it is crucial for a book such as this to be written in an open and honest manner. I speak clearly of my pain and make my struggles apparent. It is so important to discuss issues openly and honestly. To hide them contributes to the secrecy and shame that often accompany eating disorders. To share them contributes to freedom of expression and the knowledge that one is not alone.

This book follows certain guidelines. As it is intended to be non-triggering – a trigger is anything that sparks an urge to engage in eating-disordered behavior – I have limited the graphic details of my illness. I have also eliminated any mention of specific weights, calories and other related numbers from this book.

This story spans the 11 weeks I spent in residential treatment at the Renfrew Center. This is the story of my personal recovery from anorexia nervosa. I understand that other women's struggles may be very different from my own. It is therefore my hope that the description of factors common to all eating disorders, as well as the skills I have learned to deal with them, will help other women gain the hope, courage, and confidence to give up their own eating disorders and to fully recover.

At the Renfrew Center I found my voice. I learned to communicate in productive and interpersonally effective ways. I learned to be more flexible and open to life's many changes and developments. I gave up my old, negative coping skills and gained new, positive coping skills. I began the long process of finding myself. I developed the strength and courage to be who I truly am. I found self-acceptance and personal responsibility. I gained greater self-awareness and integrity. Above all, I gained the appreciation that I only have one life and I learned to make every moment count.

Introduction: Start Now

Your recovery, each moment, is up to you. An element of all-or-nothing thinking, a key cognitive distortion often accompanying eating disorders, is the belief that once a mistake occurs it's over, ruined, and if you want to do well again then you must wait until "next time." (Whether that means next semester, next week, or tomorrow is irrelevant.) Instead realize that every moment is an opportunity to begin anew. Even in the middle of a negative behavior it is possible to stop and change course.

How to

Realize that you have choices in this moment. Figure out what choices you have and which you want to make, keeping in mind the consequences. Identify negative behaviors and discontinue them. Take a moment to calm down and plan your next step. Then start now and do "the next right thing."

When to use this skill

Whenever you feel trapped in negative patterns and want a fresh new start.

*T*he first time I struggled with a full-fledged eating disorder was when I was fourteen years old. It's hard to pinpoint a cause – or even a number of causes – because so many factors were involved.

For starters, I grew up in an extremely fat-phobic home. Comments were frequently made about overweight joggers we'd see on the street, or even about overweight family members. Jokes concerning weight and body image were very common between my parents and from an early age I internalized the message that being fat was wrong and bad.

Coming from an Orthodox Jewish family, I went to a private Jewish day school from the time I was four years old. It was a small boy-heavy school with only a handful of girls in each grade. Most of the girls in my grade were small and petite. The popular girls always seemed to be the tiniest ones of all. Being a more average height for my age, I became extremely self-conscious of my size from an early age. Although I never had any weight issues, I always felt I was too big. I thought if only I was smaller people would like me better, just as they appeared to like the smaller girls. In school I surrounded myself with girls who were larger than me, hoping to feel smaller by comparison.

Despite my height concerns, I still considered myself to be thin. That is, until a few comments shattered that perception as well. In sixth grade a girl in my class told us what a certain famous gymnast weighed. I loved gymnastics and was shocked and worried that I weighed more than a gymnast. I was younger and should weigh less, I reasoned. This did not spark my eating disorder, but it planted a seed.

In eighth grade I was told by a group of friends in front of the middle school bathroom mirror that I was more "average" than "thin." That same year I looked at a photograph of my cousin's baby boy and remarked on what a cute, pudgy little baby he was. A family member commented that I "wasn't always so thin myself." Now I realize that she had been referring to the fact that I'd once been a cute, pudgy baby too, but at the time all I heard was "you're fat!" That evening I sat with a plate of macaroni and cheese and cried. It was the first time I struggled through a meal.

Eighth grade was a hard year for me and ninth grade proved no easier. The school day was long and overwhelming. I began school at eight in the morning and didn't get out until after five in the afternoon. I didn't like my classes and had few friends. One of my friends had attempted suicide and was in the hospital, severely injured. I visited her but did not know how to handle the situation in a healthy way. On top of that I was battling depression. I resorted to sleeping and self-harm to help me deal with my anxiety and as a silent cry for help. I slept through most of my classes at school and most of the time when I was at home. My mother took me for a sleep study and I was misdiagnosed with narcolepsy. I was put on a new medicine to help me stay awake. A side effect of the medication was decreased appetite. I lost weight rapidly. Around the same time, my biology class was assigned a calorie-counting project to help us learn about nutrition. That was the first time I realized how many calories were in the foods I consumed. I became obsessed. I collected lists upon lists of foods and their corresponding calories. I began to restrict the foods with the higher numbers of calories and my weight loss continued.

Despite the inherent danger, I felt quite pleased with myself. Life seemed somehow easier once I "took control" of my food consumption and weight. It felt wonderful to be good at dieting, a skill I was sure others would trade anything for!

But soon my friends began to worry. One weekend I went away on a youth group trip. I shared a room with one of the tiniest girls in my class. She was quite alarmed to discover that my clothing was smaller than hers. What I then thought was jealousy I now recognize as shock and concern.

Soon others were noticing my emaciated appearance as well. My parents realized I was in danger and began taking me to regular appointments with a therapist, psychiatrist, pediatrician, and occasionally a nutritionist. I reached a marginal level of recovery and remained there for several years. Although I was not symptom-free, I maintained a healthy weight. In fact, I was somewhat heavier than I'd ever been in my life. This did not please me. I didn't realize that I had gotten older and taller and therefore *needed* to weigh more to be healthy.

After I graduated from high school I went to study in Israel for a year at a girls' seminary in Jerusalem, as is common in Orthodox Jewish circles. When I returned home the following summer my family was very impressed by my growth and maturity. I did well in school, toured the country, lost some weight, and seemed finally to have my act together. However, my parents believed that I'd been far more independent in my achievements than I truly had been, and I didn't have the heart to explain to them otherwise. They seemed so proud of me and I wanted more of that. I decided to go back and study in Israel for another year. If one year produced such results, I could only imagine what a second year would bring!

During my first year in Israel I'd studied in a very structured school setting that essentially held my hand throughout my stay. I had help in school and with my personal growth. Every step was guided. In addition, the school was aware of my eating disorder history and made sure to watch out for my safety. I did not have the same structure or guidance during my second year.

I arrived in Israel in late August. My plan right from the start was to impress. I loved the reaction I had gotten after my first year and now I was determined to be everything everyone wanted me to be. I would learn at two schools, studying psychology and Judaic studies. I would hold down work study jobs and tour the country. I would partake in extracurricular activities and have a wonderfully rich social life. In addition, I would teach myself the third movement of Moonlight Sonata on the piano because of a comment my father had made to me to the effect that I had great piano-playing potential that I had not yet fulfilled.

I also wanted to lose some more weight. I'd gotten positive feedback when I'd lost weight the year before. People told me I looked great, some even expressed concern that I was slipping back into my anorexia. (Scary as it may seem, I took that as a compliment.) I thought that losing some weight would be the final touch. I wanted to come home more knowledgeable, more mature, more religious, more patient, more accomplished on the piano, more experienced at life and work, and thinner. I also wanted to wean myself off of the antidepressant I had taken for years. (Big mistake!) And I wanted to do it all while spending as little of my parents' time and money as possible. In short, I wanted to be "perfect." The perfect daughter, the perfect friend, the perfect student. Just perfect.

It wasn't easy, but I believed I had everything under control. I was progressing in school and in piano. I was working part-time at the student lounge and at the on-campus gym. I was traveling less often than the year before but still enough to satisfy my feeling of obligation. I participated in extracurricular activities and made many friends. All while spending virtually no money. I carefully monitored my food intake, determined to lose weight. I considered it a healthier lifestyle. I would avoid eating random foods and thereby eliminate random fat. It seemed simple enough. I was also taking a class on eating disorders in college. I couldn't possibly relapse while it was fresh on my mind, right?

Wrong.

Sometime around November I was restricting to the point that I would eventually overeat. Terrified that my mini-binges would cause weight gain I decided on a course of action. I would indulge whatever food-cravings I had for one week. After that week I assumed that all the curiosity I had about food would be gone. Once I had eaten everything I wanted to eat, the memory would be fresh on my mind and I wouldn't crave food anymore. I'd have the memories to keep me satisfied! I hoped I'd remember the self-disgust I felt upon eating "bad foods," and therefore keep away from them in the future.

For one week, during Hanukah, I ate many foods I craved. I did not fully indulge, but I did overeat to some extent. After the week ended I went back to restriction. I first cut out foods containing fat. Oily foods, fried foods, and greasy foods were "bad foods." I also cut out foods with added sugar. No candy, cookies, donuts, or fruit drinks. If I had a question about whether a food was "edible" I erred on the side of "safety" and assumed that it was not. If ever I felt tempted to eat a "bad food" I reminded myself of a comment someone made to me after a trip to the beach. She told me that she was shocked to see I had such a "full woman figure" when I "looked so thin with clothes on." It was generally enough to fuel my restriction. (At the time, however, I remarked to someone that the girl was lucky to have made the comment to *me* since *I* could handle it, and that she should be more careful, as she could easily have made the comment to a girl with an eating disorder instead!) A dorm counselor told me what a blessing it was to be thin nearly every time she saw me. I felt good.

My weight began to drop but not as quickly as I would have liked. So I cut out starchy foods such as bread, muffins, and pasta from my diet. Ironically I still ate oatmeal. (Eating disorders are not known for their sound reasoning!) Soon I was restricting virtually all foods. But in a dorm where one girl believed that white bread poisoned people and another girl had a sculpture of dried bananas instead of a birthday cake, my disordered eating went unnoticed. I found that while I controlled my eating and my weight, everything else seemed less important. Suddenly it seemed I could tolerate the stresses of school and work and money management. It was like magic – for a very short time.

Soon it was winter. Israel does not typically see snow but that year Jerusalem got about two inches. It shut down the city buses, schools, and businesses. Construction cranes were out on the roads scraping at the streets. People shook umbrellas at the falling snow, or else tried to sweep it away with kitchen brooms. The city was unprepared for such weather.

My dorm building was also ill-equipped to handle the "brutal" winter. The snow got inside the roof and seeped down into the walls. There was a lot of leaking, dripping, water damage, and mold. In a dorm with limited heating and hot water, this was bad news. People began to get sick, myself included. But as the cleanup progressed, the other girls regained their health. I got sicker, my immunity down due to my eating disorder.

I came down with what I thought was the flu. I ran a high fever and my whole body ached. I was freezing cold and miserable. Soon I realized that I wasn't healing in my cold and dirty dorm room so I went to my cousins' house across the country in the hopes of getting better there. I was put on an antibiotic to help control my flu. I lost my appetite almost completely. I ate virtually nothing that week and my weight plummeted. A week later my fever subsided and, feeling somewhat better, I returned to school.

The first thing I noticed was that it was hard to stand on the bus anymore. I had to sit or else I lost my balance. It took me a long time to walk places. Stairs were extremely difficult to climb. I felt so weak.

When I arrived at school I was met by the shocked face of a dorm counselor. She told me that I'd gotten extremely thin since she'd last seen me. She said it didn't look good, and that I needed to gain some weight and fast. I felt so flattered that she noticed my weight loss. But I was starting to wonder if my weakness was connected to my weight loss and by this point I agreed that logically I did need to gain weight. I felt so superior that *my* weight issue was the need to *gain* weight! How many people can boast of that? I assured her that my weight loss was simply due to my weeklong flu. I told her I was confident that I would regain any lost weight. But when I went to the cafeteria for lunch that day I found it impossible to eat. I looked at the food. Nothing seemed edible. It was all oily and greasy and full of sugar and starch! I couldn't even eat the soup anymore! Nothing followed my rules, not even the salads! Finally I found some plain chopped vegetables. There were peppers. I firmly believed that the calorie content of peppers depended on their color. I erroneously believed that the calorie content increased as the pepper evolved from green to yellow to orange to red. So I ate only the green peppers. I felt so trapped and alone.

I realized that this had gone far enough. I wanted to be able to eat again, but it was too late. As my eating became increasingly disordered, I ceased eating in the cafeteria with others. Instead I ate alone in my dorm, that is, when I *did* happen to eat. Eating alone made it easier to avoid others' judgment. I think people knew I was in trouble by this point. The dorm mother called my parents to alert them as to what was going on. I assured everyone that I was okay. I knew what I was doing, trust me!

But soon even I knew I was out of control. I could only eat oatmeal, plain yogurt, green vegetables, and apples. I often refused to drink tea due to the few calories it contained, preferring instead to drink hot water to warm myself. Yet despite the obvious illogic, I believed I was just being "healthier," and "more careful" with what I put into my body. The lack of clutter in my body would clear me out, make me more focused, exercise better, and just be overall a better, more in-control person. When I ate, I ate alone and in total silence. Before I would even consider eating, my entire apartment had to be immaculately clean. I left the table several times to exercise during my "meals." Even when I had no energy for anything else, I forced myself into the shower to exercise as it was the only place I felt warm enough. I never ate after seven at night. I chewed gum and drank ridiculous amounts of water to keep from feeling hungry. I cut my food into miniscule pieces and mixed foods into strange and inappropriate combinations in order to experience every possible combination. I was literally starving and therefore no food tasted bad to me. Mixing foods that don't go well together is often a sign of an eating disorder and is common among those suffering from anorexia. I smelled every bite before tasting it. I became obsessed with collecting recipes and cooking food for others, but never eating any myself. I compared my food intake and body image to that of others. I ate "vicariously" by watching others eat. I spat out most of the food I supposedly "ate."

My dorm counselor stopped telling me that it was a blessing to be thin. Most of the time, I was too weak to attend school. Many days I opted to lie in bed and sleep simply because I was too weak to climb stairs. I slept to avoid hunger and pain and cold. I looked forward to nothing. My thoughts were consumed with food. I was depressed and cried at the most seemingly random triggers, often unable to stop crying for long periods of time. I slowly stopped functioning to the best of my ability. My thinking became increasingly hazy and distorted. Soon I was unable to function in any sort of healthy way. My life was unmanageable. And yet I still believed that I did not have an eating disorder because I "knew" I could stop at any time. I was just waiting for the right moment. But right moments came and went and nothing changed.

Six months after my arrival in Israel I had become critically ill, and by February practically all I could do was lie in bed and sleep, half-listening to music. I survived minute to minute, hour to hour, but I was not living. February was the longest month of my entire life (which is ironic, February being the shortest month and all). I was miserable.

I couldn't walk well or do stairs reliably. My body hurt all the time. Winter began to end but I couldn't feel the warmth. I was ice cold no matter how hot it was. My hands and feet were a deathly grayish-blue and my fingernails were purple. Soon it was March and I still had a blister on my foot from September. My period stopped a while back but rather than believe that it was due to my severely low body weight, I went to doctors and specialists to try and "solve the mystery." By the time I realized what was happening all I could do was lie in bed, day after day, often without the energy to turn myself over from a cramped position. I lacked the energy to blow my nose. I had accidents like a toddler. Socks cut off circulation to my feet. I couldn't lift my arms above my head, even to brush my hair, without risking fainting. I rarely left bed. I listened to my iPod and slept for more and more hours each day. I was dying.

I have often heard about the concept of one's life passing before one's eyes. For me it came in the form of romanticized childhood memories. Whenever I had the energy to get out of bed I sat for hours on the computer, emailing fragmented sentences describing happy childhood memories to my sister. I often lived in another world – I was lost in a world of happy memories, a perfect world of simple joy – a world that did not exist. My mother says that when she saw those emails she knew I was in serious danger.

I sometimes wondered if the next time I fell asleep I wouldn't wake up, but it didn't scare me. In a vague sense I knew what was happening to me: my body was shutting down. But it felt like I was just falling asleep. Like death was just extended sleep. In a way I knew it wasn't too far off but I was too tired to care anymore. Nothing felt important. I had no energy left to live. I was barely surviving. But most of the time I was too tired to realize that I was dying. I just thought I was losing my sense of idealism, that I just didn't care about anything anymore and was becoming a cold, uncaring member of the adult world. I disliked myself for that. I couldn't think. I'd stare a lot. I started to feel like "a starving animal." I got rough around the edges. People would come to visit me and I'd just tell them to leave. I had no energy left for smiles or social grace. I managed to isolate myself while living in a tiny room with two other girls!

My roommates and the other girls in my apartment knew I wasn't well but didn't know why. I told them that even I didn't know what was wrong with me. I suspect my two roommates, Leslie and Carla, were aware of my eating disorder even if they did not realize the full extent of the dangers involved.

One evening, Leslie entered the room while I spoke with my mother on the phone about my struggles with food. I was very distraught and didn't manage to change the subject in time to prevent Leslie from hearing the conversation. Nevertheless I "explained" to Leslie afterwards that she hadn't heard the conversation correctly and proceeded to tell her that someone in my family was having issues and that I was okay. She assured me that it was none of her business and that she wouldn't share my private matters with anyone.

It was harder to hide my struggles from Carla. Her mother struggled with an eating disorder and Carla recognized some of the warning signs. I made her promise she wouldn't tell anyone. I told her that if the school found out I could be kicked out and sent home. If I decided to go home and seek help I wanted it to be *my* decision.

I wanted to stay in Israel and stick it out to the end of the year. I wanted to finish what I started. I even wanted to stay longer and work on a summer program for high school students. But I soon realized that I was in grave danger and needed to come home early.

It was not an easy decision in the least. I agonized back and forth for many weeks. I worried I would hate myself forever for bringing my study in Israel to an early end. I worried that my health would further deteriorate if I stayed longer. I worried that if I went home early I would be a miserable failure and never amount to anything. I worried that I wasn't "sick enough" or "thin enough" to seek help for an eating disorder. I thought I should be strong enough to heal on my own and I judged myself harshly for needing help.

In the end what made my decision was that I couldn't bear the thought of staying any longer. I was deep in anguish. Each moment felt like an eternity. I looked at my calendar and wept.

I hesitantly spoke with my father and we decided together that a good time to come home early was just after Passover, a few weeks away. A few weeks, in my present state, seemed an unbearably long time to wait. My mother's entire extended family was coming for Passover and I didn't want them to see me so sick. But I desperately wanted to be home. A few moments after we hung up, I called my father back.

"I want to come home," I said, "as soon as I possibly can." Once I said it I wanted it more than ever. My father booked me a flight home on Monday, four days away. I called my aunt in Israel with whom I'd stayed earlier in my relapse and arranged to stay with her again until my flight home. Before I left for the United States she asked me a serious question.

"Why don't you just eat?"

I answered honestly, "I don't know."

I arrived home on March 13, 2007. My mother cried when she saw me. I assumed it was because she was so happy to see me. The following day, my twentieth birthday, my mother took me to see Dr. Bridget, a pediatrician at the Cleveland Clinic.

I arrived at the Cleveland Clinic for my appointment and was greeted by a nurse who instructed me to undress, put on a hospital gown, and come to the scale. I did as I was told. When the nurse would not tell me my weight, however, I became distraught.

"I did not come home to be treated like this," I told my mother. "I did not sign on for this..." I was extremely upset at not having been told my weight and I disliked what I considered to be the nurse's mistrust of me. I ranted on and on about it, saying that I doubted Dr. Bridget could possibly help me. I was angry with the nurse for "treating me like a baby" and because I assumed everyone at the Cleveland Clinic would treat me the same way, I was angry with them all. I was all set to hate Dr. Bridget when she walked into the room.

I loved her immediately. We talked for a very long time. Dr. Bridget asked me a lot of basic medical questions and then many questions about my eating-disordered behavior. She asked me about my "eating disorder voice," which I defensively countered was "not an actual voice." Dr. Bridget assured me she understood exactly what I meant. She really seemed to understand eating disorders. She made me feel as though she truly understood what I was going through and how I was thinking. She validated my thoughts and feelings and for the first time I felt less alone.

After a physical examination she determined that I required hospitalization. My heart was unstable to the point of heart failure. I had a severe pulse deficit. My heart rate and blood pressure were dangerously low. I was to begin the refeeding process, which can be dangerous, even fatal, in the hospital under careful supervision. I would take medication to help my body develop the ability to digest food once again. Dr. Bridget told me that I was lucky to have come for help when I did. Given another week or two, it well could have been too late. Dr. Bridget stayed late in order to ensure me a bed in the M-30 wing of the children's hospital, the best wing for my condition. Dr. Bridget would not see me during my hospital stay, as she would be on vacation, but she called several times to check on me. I felt so cared for. I loved Dr. Bridget.

I spent the following two and a half weeks on full bed rest in the hospital. I was allowed out of bed – with assistance – only to use my bedside commode and to be weighed in the morning. I was not allowed to know my weight for the duration of my stay in the hospital. At first I was furious. "That is *my* number," I demanded of every doctor and nurse who dared to enter my room, "and I *need* to know it!" But soon I found that not knowing my weight gave me one less thing to stress over in my recovery and I came to view the not knowing as a positive thing.

I had 24/7 supervision via a bedside sitter. Every meal was carefully measured out and timed. I had thirty minutes to complete each meal and fifteen minutes to complete each snack. Oftentimes Ensure, a dietary supplement, was required to help keep me from losing weight as I entered a hypermetabolic state. These were typically added to my meals or snacks. Eventually my caloric needs dictated that I consume a quantity of food requiring more time than my allotted thirty minutes. After some debate, I was granted an extra fifteen minutes per meal.

When I was first admitted to the hospital it felt surreal. I thought everyone was overreacting. I couldn't possibly be as sick as they all thought I was! Doctors talked to me about heart failure and I broke out into giggles. I wasn't that sick! But in truth, I sensed that something was in fact wrong. I knew I'd been feeling dangerously ill lately and the chest pains scared me. I would later learn that a few episodes of dizzy, numb, tingling and throbbing in my chest had most likely been heart arrhythmias. Nevertheless I was afraid that at any moment someone would barge into my room and demand that I leave, claiming that I was not really so sick after all and I should make room in the hospital for people who need it.

That never happened. Every doctor who crossed my path seemed pretty concerned for my safety and well-being. Each day I met with a wonderful nutritionist named Tara. On the first day she came into my room and left me a menu, asking me to fill out my food choices for the next day. She said she'd be back at three in the afternoon to pick it up from me. I sat with that menu from 10:00 am to 3:00 pm and all I determined was that "sometime tomorrow I would like a blueberry yogurt."

My thinking was so hazy that I had trouble keeping up in even the simplest of conversations. Doctors and nurses had to go over things many times, very slowly, in order for me to grasp what they were saying. And then they had to remind me what was said later. I had many of the same conversations with my doctors each day. Often I felt as though we'd discussed something similar before, but I couldn't quite remember. My thinking had become so foggy and sedated that I often found it difficult to string two words together. I could no longer read books or magazines – by the time I reached the end of a sentence I forgot the beginning! Nothing seemed to make much sense. So it was little wonder my menus took so much out of me.

Tara came back at three and went over the menu with me to help me make some sensible choices – choices that would include more than one item per day. She told me she would work with me and that soon I'd be filling out menus like a pro. Weeks later we were still going through each food item, reviewing its exchanges (a system where we would count exchanges of various nutrient groups rather than calories. A certain number of grams of a nutrient, such as protein, equaled one exchange) and debating which meal it went best with. Luckily Tara didn't mind my food rituals. In fact, no one raised any objections when I decided that it was a good idea to make tiny cream cheese sandwiches out of bran flakes and dip them in juice. They were just pleased I was eating.

During each meal I had my bedside sitter close my curtain, and remove my phone. I required absolute silence. I carefully unwrapped each and every food item before I allowed the timing to begin. Everything had to be closely examined and cleaned. Forks and spoons underwent especially careful inspection. I began by smelling each of the food items separately. I then cut the foods into tiny pieces and mixed them with each other. As I was used to eating very little, I wanted to experience every possible combination and savor the moment. I went through many napkins, as I often used my fingers to mix my food. I ate unreasonably slowly. I dragged out each meal to the last minute, terrified that if I finished even a second early it would indicate a lack of control over my food, and that if given the chance I would eat until I cleared out the kitchen!

As the refeeding process continued I entered into a hypermetabolic state. When I was first admitted, the room was set on 90 degrees Fahrenheit and I still felt freezing cold. Now I was having hot flashes! I was scared to tell anyone because, not knowing much about the refeeding process, I assumed they'd think that since I was no longer miserably cold I must be all better now. I was afraid that they might send me home prematurely. That fear, too, was unfounded.

I didn't have to tell anyone about my hot flashes because my night sweats were hard to miss. Each night I woke up literally drenched in sweat. I was cramping and bloated and sweaty and felt worse than ever. My doctors assured me it was a good sign. I didn't see how that could possibly be true, but they hadn't been wrong yet, so I believed them.

Before I came to the hospital I hardly ate anything. I was afraid of most foods I was required to eat. I was especially afraid of anything sugary, as I'd been craving sugar more than ever in my life and I was afraid that if I started eating sweets I would never want to stop. But as I integrated more and more sugary foods into my diet, such as ice cream and cookies, I slowly began to crave them less and less. Feeling more normalized, I was relieved to discover that eating half a cup of ice cream did not mean that I would finish the carton!

When I neared discharge, Tara had me make a comprehensive list of foods I wanted to incorporate into my diet when I went home. She said to include every food I'd ever eaten, currently eat, or planned to eat in the future. Then we reviewed the exchanges in each. There were hundreds upon hundreds of foods on my list. And all this on top of the hours spent agonizing over the same menu day after day for weeks. Tara had the patience of a saint!

I was discharged shortly before Passover. I was to attend a day program at the Cleveland Center for Eating Disorders (CCED) for an indefinite amount of time. My rabbi declared it a matter of life or death for me to attend treatment and as such I was permitted to ride to treatment even during the holiday. This, more than anything, impressed upon me the seriousness of my condition.

My first day at CCED will not soon be forgotten by those who witnessed it. I arrived at 12:00 noon on April 3, 2007.

I panicked when Maddie the coordinator of the day program weighed me, because I had just eaten and was wearing a lot of clothing. I had been up the night before, worrying that CCED would not know how to measure my weight and vitals, and here I was and it seemed to be true! How could they weigh me with my clothes on after I'd just eaten? The number would be wrong! What if they saw the higher number and decided that I wasn't sick enough to be in treatment? I worked myself into a panic. I cried and blew up at Maddie for the first time of many. Luckily, she was just as bubbly as ever and didn't fight me back and the whole thing blew over quickly.

Then came orientation which was really frustrating because I was also supposed to be eating lunch. But there were two other people there (Maddie and another new patient) and there was also no table. I couldn't focus on orientation *and* on eating. Especially without a table! I was very anxious and just couldn't seem to do it. Maddie kept reminding me that I had to eat, which didn't help anything, so instead of focusing on orientation or eating, all I could think was "I can't eat, I can't eat!" And then I really couldn't eat. And I cried again. When orientation was over and I'd absorbed almost nothing from it, we went to join the group. Maddie first tried to hold up the group while I ate. I felt trapped and said I needed the bathroom. Afterwards Maddie let me sit and finish eating at the table alone while the group continued with its planned activity. That helped and I was able to eat.

By dinner, I had been feeling faint and dizzy all day and it was getting worse. A few times I nearly fell over. I stood up to get napkins at dinner and fainted. That freaked everyone out. I kept saying that I was okay, but they didn't believe me and the head of the program, Dr. Andrews, wondered if I should go back to the hospital. Eventually I went back to the group. It was quite a day.

Thankfully not every day at CCED was as eventful as my first. After that first day things settled down a bit. I attended treatment at CCED for six hours a day, five days a week. Although at first it appeared to be helping, I struggled significantly in my treatment at CCED. Being in charge of packing my own food often proved too much of a challenge. Each day I spent hours upon hours in the kitchen counting and measuring out food, trying desperately to pack meals for the following day.

I was still too brain starved to participate much in group therapy during the day. Mostly I sat and stared, listening but forgetting most of what was said only moments later. Unable to think well, I didn't have the mental capacity to argue and I appeared compliant.

Pretty soon it all changed. As I ate and more nutrition entered my body, I began to experience clearer thinking. My first thoughts were, "what am I doing?" and "treatment is ruining everything I've worked for!" No longer could I be called a compliant patient. I was unruly and disruptive. I argued that I did not actually have a true eating disorder. And I *believed* that I didn't have an eating disorder! I believed that I could stop at any time and that I just didn't *want* to stop. I went back and forth a lot. Sometimes I knew I needed help. Sometimes I wanted to get better. Other times I wanted to fight treatment. Sometimes even when I wanted help I fought my treatment team. Logically I knew that my thinking was distorted. On April 5, 2007, I wrote in my journal:

> It's no game but it feels like one. It's like I can't trust anything I think anymore. Suddenly it's "no big deal" that I could die or never have children. Logically I know that's terrible stuff. But there is this major disconnect in my mind... All my life it was my biggest aspiration to be a mom. I didn't always know what I wanted to be professionally or what I wanted to study, but I *always* wanted to be a mom. And now it's like, "okay, no big deal." Logically I know something is wrong, but it's so far away. Everything feels so far away.

Initially the more mental energy I acquired, the more apparent the distortions in my thinking became. By April 7, I was convinced that I'd gained back all the weight I'd ever need. I wrote in my journal that "Dr. Bridget is going to be shocked that I actually did this...I reached maintenance weight in just a few days! It's not all evenly distributed yet, but I figure in another few days that'll be there too." I had been on blind weight, not aware of my weight, since my first day in the hospital. But since I believed that I'd reached my ideal body weight, despite the fact that I was still dangerously underweight, I took comments such as "you look good" or "you look much better" to mean "you look fat" or "you put on enough padding to outweigh the Goodyear blimp!"

It wasn't long before I started to create serious conflict in my nutritionist's office and beyond. We worked on the exchange system, which wound up playing to my weakness. In my head the whole thing became a twisted number game. Since I was still in a hypermetabolic state, my food plan had to be monitored very closely. Once I believed I was becoming too heavy and I started keeping to the bare minimums of my food plan, I lost weight once again. Although I was not told the specific numbers, I was told that my weight had begun a downward trend. I experienced a warped sense of satisfaction upon hearing this news. Wanting to keep the downward weight trend going, I fought my nutritionist at CCED over every exchange. Each time she tried to increase my food plan I threw a fit, crying and saying that if she increased my food plan I would stop eating completely.

Dr. Andrews tried to get me to accept medication, which he believed would help me recover at a faster pace. I continually refused it, stating that I didn't have a true eating disorder and that I definitely did not need medication! I believed that medication would alter my mind and that I wouldn't be myself anymore. I believed that accepting medication meant declaring, "I am not good enough by myself. I need medication to alter my brain chemistry and make me a different person." There was no *way* I wanted to give that message to *anyone*! I was also afraid of *how* the medication might change me. I wanted to work through my issues in a legitimate, real way. I didn't want any help. I thought that getting help was cheating. If I took medication to recover, how could I ever be certain I could do this on my own? I might relapse when I stopped taking the medicine! Eventually I was put on a low dose of a medicine for one week. When it didn't immediately solve all of my problems (and it caused drowsiness) I declared it ineffective and stopped taking it.

Unable to function well in group and noncompliant with my treatment team, the idea of residential eating disorder treatment came up time and time again. I knew that my current level of treatment was not working for me and I wanted to try residential. But I didn't know how to *say* that I needed more help. So instead I acted out. I restricted, I cut corners in treatment, and I *showed* everyone how miserable I was. I did everything in my power to act out the message, "I need to go into residential treatment!" This resulted in major conflict both in my family and at CCED.

My last few days at CCED, much like my first day, were memorable. I fought with staff over my meals and I often refused to eat at all. I struggled with food rituals and couldn't understand why they cared what and how I was eating, as long as I ate. I wasn't trying to cause trouble. I felt so stuck and I didn't know any other way to communicate that I needed more help than CCED could offer me. On several occasions I cried hysterically, becoming virtually unresponsive. It wasn't long before I was asked to leave the program and seek a higher level of care in a residential setting. Knowing a few people who had come through Renfrew and were doing well, I chose the Renfrew Center. A week later I was on a plane to Florida.

1
Week One: Be Honest

Honesty means more than simply telling the truth. It requires sincerity and openness. Eating disorders thrive on manipulation and secrets. In order to recover you must be honest first and foremost with yourself. Only then can you extend your honesty to others.

How to

It is not easy to admit you need help, but it is a crucial first step. Make a commitment to honesty. Be open with those who can support you, beginning this moment. Don't hide information or keep secrets. Don't manipulate or play games. Be upfront and truthful. Remember that a lie by omission is still a lie. Sincerity is key. If you find yourself lacking confidence or motivation to recover, discuss it with those who can guide you.

When to use this skill

When you work toward recovery. Throughout the treatment process. When you wish to make lasting changes.

*J*looked around the Florida Room. It was bright and sunny with couches arranged in a square. There was a rug in the center of the room covering a stone floor. There were several boxes of tissues on every conceivable surface. At the far end of the room were a table and a mini refrigerator containing snacks. My mother asked if I wanted a snack and when I refused she insisted I eat the fruit cup she'd packed with her. My mother and I sat on the couch facing a window overlooking a dolphin-shaped swimming pool. Across from us sat Maureen, the woman who would lead our orientation. We began with the necessary paperwork. I dated everything Thursday May 17, 2007, and signed my name.

Maureen told us that Renfrew was divided into two teams: the red team and the blue team. Although the patients on each team interacted on a daily basis, the teams helped divide the patients into smaller sections for therapy groups and activities. Therapists, nutritionists, psychiatrists, and aftercare staff were also divided into teams, each working with patients on his or her team. I was assigned to the red team.

Maureen also explained that Renfrew worked on a level system. There were several levels, each with corresponding privileges. The levels represented status and were a very big deal amongst the patients at Renfrew. I would begin on level one. There were not only levels above level one, but below it as well. The levels were: full day room, partial day room, level one, level two, level three, and level four. Every Tuesday each patient on the red team attended "team rounds" where she was evaluated for a level change. The blue team met on Wednesdays.

I looked at Maureen. She had brown hair pulled up in a ponytail. She seemed a decent size. Or was she? Was she thinner than me? Prettier than me? Did Maureen think I looked sick enough to be at Renfrew? Was I thin enough? Frail-looking enough? She probably thought I could stand to lose some more weight. I tried not to think about it. I continued signing the many contracts and forms.

A few moments later a young girl walked in with two women who introduced themselves as her mother and aunt. The girl's name was Melanie. I scrutinized her. Was Melanie thinner than me? Taller than me? Prettier than me? She was sixteen years old but looked somewhat mature for her age. She had short, choppy, highlighted hair and wore heavy eye makeup. She was very pretty. Prettier than me? What did *she* think about the way I looked? What did her family think? Maybe my fears were true. Maybe no one thought I looked sick enough to come to Renfrew!

My thoughts were interrupted by my stomach growling. I hadn't eaten yet today. I thought that Renfrew, a residential eating disorder treatment facility, would require me to eat. I told my mother that if I ate before I came it would be more difficult to make a good first impression and eat at Renfrew. By now we all realized that had been a foolish decision and I knew that it had been a manipulation. I hadn't wanted to eat and I said anything that would convince my mother that I shouldn't eat. Now it would be more difficult to eat here, surrounded by these strangers. I worried that if I ate on my first day they might think I wasn't sick enough to be here. What if Renfrew sent me home, after all my hard work and traveling to get here? I pretended not to notice my rumbling stomach and hoped others wouldn't either.

But it was too late. My mother noticed and once again asked me to eat the fruit cup. I didn't want to make a scene, and I really *was* hungry, so I ate a piece of diced peach. Then I stopped. *Melanie* wasn't eating anything. Why should

I be eating? Everyone would be watching me eat and think to themselves, "Why is Naomi eating? Doesn't she know where she *is*? If she can eat now, she can eat at home too. She doesn't need to be here!" They would see my size – I unrealistically considered myself to be far larger than I was – and see me eating and put two and two together. I abruptly put away the fruit cup but it continued to monopolize my thoughts as orientation continued.

Maureen explained that a typical day at Renfrew began at roughly 6:00 am with a trip to the nurses for vital signs. Those who were medically cleared for exercise had the opportunity to do so during the exercise group at 6:30 am. At around 7:00 am residents picked a number and stood in line for their medications. Breakfast began at 8:00 am.

Most of the day was spent in group therapy sessions. There were many, many different kinds of groups. In art therapy we would create art projects to help us express our thoughts and feelings and to learn new ways to communicate. In cinema therapy we would watch videos and discuss issues and themes that come up in each film. During psychodrama we would have the opportunity to role play and explore challenging relationships. Other groups targeted self-esteem issues or taught new coping skills such as interpersonal effectiveness and assertiveness.

After our morning groups was lunch at 12:00 noon. The after-meal support group was held immediately afterward at 1:00 pm. Between 1:00 pm and 6:00 pm were more groups and various appointments with nutritionists and therapists. Dinner was at 6:00 pm and evening wrap up was at 7:00 pm and ran until 8:15 pm. Scattered throughout the day were snack and medication times.

On Saturdays there was a multifamily therapy group between 9:30 am and 11:00 am to which all family members of Renfrew residents were invited. Following the group was a therapy session exclusively for the family members while the residents attended a team building session. Also on Saturdays was a special group called "excursion" during which the patients on levels three and four were taken on trips to learn to deal with real-life experiences that can pose challenges for women struggling with eating disorders – such as eating popcorn at the movies or going clothing shopping.

Maureen continued explaining the rules and regulations of Renfrew. Soon the paperwork was completed. My mom went with Maureen for a tour and I went to meet with a nurse for a physical examination. The nurse took my pulse and blood pressure and asked me a variety of questions. She took my picture for her files. I worried about how my picture looked and what others would think of it. I asked to see my photograph but the nurse would not show it to me. She explained that many girls who come to Renfrew have similar concerns about their pictures. I wasn't thrilled but I understood.

After the nursing assessment I was shown to my room, A-9. It was a nice-sized room on the first floor. The wall opposite the door had large windows looking out on a green lawn frequented by iguanas. There was a door leading to a bathroom shared with the room next door. Mounted on the bathroom door was a full-length mirror. In the room were two closets, two chairs, two laundry baskets and two beds, one closer to the window and one closer to the door. The bed by the door was to be mine. It was covered by a flowery bedspread and a set of towels. To the right of the bed stood a nightstand containing three large drawers. On top of the nightstand were a lamp and a box of tissues. There seemed to be tissues everywhere at this place!

Two staff members brought in my suitcase and backpack, which had both been taken from me upon arrival. They went through my things, searching for "contraband." In the end they took my sunscreen and mouthwash because they contained alcohol in the first three ingredients. They also took my razors, nail clipper, and tweezers because they were sharp items. Since I have a history of self-harm, I was on "sharps-restriction," which essentially meant that this was the last time I would see my sharp things for a while.

After they left I began to reorganize and put away my things. Just then, a girl with stunningly gorgeous red hair walked in and introduced herself as Faith. She was my roommate for approximately five minutes. As I unpacked my things, she gathered her things to move rooms. We chatted for a few moments. I told her I'd been studying in Israel this past year and she mentioned that she wanted to go to Israel for an archeology project. It felt good to have a common bond with someone already, even if she was moving.

Just then, before I could finish unpacking, Andrea, the psychiatric nurse practitioner, called me for my psychiatric evaluation. We walked to an empty office and sat down. It was a small room. We sat across from each other and the interview began. She asked me several questions about my medical and psychiatric history, as well as the development of my eating disorder. I was as open and truthful as possible.

I told Andrea about my struggles with anorexia. I told her about my initial battle at age fourteen and my relapse at age nineteen. I shared with Andrea my treatment experiences in the hospital and at CCED leading up to my admission to Renfrew.

Andrea asked me several follow-up questions. We discussed my fear of medication. I told her that I was completely against taking medication. I didn't want any "help" from drugs. I wanted to do the work on my own. If I took medicine, how could I ever know if my recovery was due to my work or due to the medicine? I refused medication.

We also discussed lunch: pizza and veggies, which had come at the beginning of our meeting and was now sitting cold on the table.

"You were never going to eat that, were you?" she asked me.

"No, I wasn't," I admitted. I thought to myself that I *couldn't* eat it – especially not in the middle of the story of my eating disorder. How would that look? If I was to eat, I would completely invalidate my whole story! Then Andrea would think I wasn't sick enough to be here. I kept waiting for her to "make me" eat, but she never did. Renfrew tries not to pressure people on their first day.

The meeting ended and I went back to my room to finish unpacking before my meeting with a Renfrew nutritionist at 3:00 pm. Since it was a Thursday Jackie, my nutritionist, was not in. (She doesn't work at Renfrew on Thursdays.) I would meet Jackie tomorrow. Today I saw Trish, another red team nutritionist.

I met with Trish at around 3:00 pm. I sat across from her in her office as she introduced herself and handed me a menu. She asked me to select foods from several categories to make up a meal. I stared intently at the menu. I hadn't eaten a proper meal in so long and I wanted the meal to be perfect. I was also terrified that if I chose the "wrong foods" I would gain too much weight. I was so afraid of gaining weight and appearing as though I was "all better" before I truly was. I decided that initially I should play it "safe" and choose low-calorie foods. As I sat trying to determine my meal, Trish grew impatient. It had been nearly forty-five minutes and I hadn't made any headway towards choosing any food items. When she tried to help me "just choose food," I cried. I wanted this to be *perfect*. Didn't she understand? Finally Trish took the menu from me and gave me only a few choices. Would I like almonds or walnuts, for example? This sped up the process significantly. Unable to simply circle foods on a menu, it was little wonder that I'd struggled to pack my own meals during my days at CCED. Our session ended and I left the room, emotionally drained.

By this point in the day I was exhausted and overwhelmed by all the new information.

Worn out, I went back to my room and lay down. Faith had already gone. She moved upstairs, a privilege for those who were progressing in their recoveries. The rooms upstairs were larger and had skylights in the bathrooms.

I must have fallen asleep because the next thing I knew it was dinner time. Most of the Renfrew community eats in the dining room. But since I struggled so much during meals it was determined that I should eat in the community room, a place for those who needed extra support.

The community room was at the end of the hallway on the first floor. The wood ceiling was sloped and pretty. Two ceiling fans hung down from either side of the room. On each side of the room was a set of large windows looking out onto a porch. One was the smoke porch. The other was the fresh air porch. Most of the room was filled with couches and chairs. Along the back wall was a cushioned bench. There were games and puzzles, arts and crafts, and a television. On the left side of the room there was a refrigerator and microwave. There was also a long table with many chairs around it. This was where I would eat dinner.

Renfrew had many rules governing the eating of a meal. I was to keep my eyes on my own plate, not discuss weights, calories, or other related numbers, finish on time, and use no food rituals. I came to Renfrew with many, many food rituals. I cut my food into pieces, I mixed foods into inappropriate combinations – the list goes on. In order to make things easier for me in the beginning, I was told to simply worry about finishing my meal on time. I would work on food rituals later.

I walked towards the table. There were a few women already seated for the meal. One of them I recognized as Melanie, the girl I met during orientation. The others I did not know. At the head of the table was a psych-tech whose job it was to provide assistance to patients during the meal.

She seemed friendly enough. I sat down. Since I keep kosher, my meal came prepackaged. I opened it and froze, staring horrified at my food. I was supposed to eat *this*?! I gaped at my hamburger and fries as if they were from another planet. By my reaction you'd think that they were asking me to eat something terrible, like road kill or sewer sludge. I began to cry.

I cried and cried, and no one could calm me down. I thought that coming into residential treatment would be the magical cure for my disorder. I hadn't eaten anything all day and now there was perfectly good food in front of me and I just couldn't eat it! My mind raced with all the reasons why the hamburger was not actually edible. *It has fat in it! The fries will cause weight gain! The bun is too thick! Don't eat, don't eat, don't eat!* I looked around at the other girls who had already begun their meals. The psych-tech asked how she could support me. I only cried harder. I didn't know how anyone could help me when I didn't even know what kind of help I needed! I thought I was just waiting for the right moment to be "cured" but even when I *wanted* to eat I found that I could not. I firmly believed that in order to succeed in treatment I had to be perfect, to make no mistakes whatsoever. I believed that once a mistake was made it was "over" and there was no fixing it. I considered my delay in eating a mistake. I thought if only I had started the meal on time with the others I would be fine, but now it was too late. I would never recover. It was very black and white.

I took out a fork and began to pick at my food. Melanie mentioned that I was triggering her and asked me to please eat more normally. That was that last straw. If I couldn't eat the way I wanted to eat, then I wouldn't eat at all! Now I had the perfect excuse: Melanie upset me. It was no longer my fault! I no longer had to try to eat. I stormed away from the table in tears, lying down in the corner on the floor between the bench in the back of the room and the window facing the smoke porch. The psych-tech came over to me.

I told her flatly, "I am going to die here."

"Why do you say that?" she asked. She was kind and sweet but I couldn't seem to find the right words to express what I needed to express. So instead I continued to make it about the food.

"Because if I can't eat here I can't eat anywhere!" I sobbed. But despite my worries, in my mind I was secretly pleased with the way the evening was going. I had been so worried that no one would think I was sick enough to warrant residential treatment. Now I was pretty sure they would be convinced of the seriousness of my situation.

After each meal I was supposed to fill out a food journal for Jackie, my nutritionist. On it I was to record what I ate and my moods, thoughts, and feelings related to my meal. I sat down and wrote: "I am really, *really* sad, anxious, [and] frustrated...I hate this!"

After I had finished making a scene in the community room, I went back to my room and cried. I couldn't seem to stop crying. I was angry and frustrated and desperately wanted someone to hold my hand and tell me everything would be okay. I felt so alone. I curled up in a ball beside my bed and cried hysterically. Sharon, a counselor, came in to check on me a while later and found me on the floor crying. She asked me what was wrong. She tried to talk to me but I remained unresponsive, other than to glare at her, trying to communicate somehow through my eyes. I didn't know how to express what it was that I needed. Finally I told her that I still hadn't eaten yet today. She asked if I wanted to try a nutritional supplement drink called Boost. She said that if I drank a Boost my treatment team would see that I really did want to get better.

Suddenly I began to worry in the opposite direction. From Sharon I gathered that Renfrew *did* see how sick I was. Now I began to worry that they would think I was *too* sick! I felt as if the entire thing was under my control, and that I was playing some sort of game, trying to be the perfect amount of "sick." I wanted help. I *needed* help. But I didn't know any way to get help other than by acting out on my eating disorder symptoms. Now it seemed I was getting some support. I accepted Sharon's offer and we went back to the community room together.

Earlier in the day I mentioned to a staff member that I hadn't eaten anything yet and the staff member offered me a snack in the community room. By the time we got there, however, I changed my mind and was too afraid to have a snack. The same thing happened with the Boost.

"What flavor would you like?" Sharon asked me, reaching into the refrigerator.

"Umm..." I stammered. This was a bad idea. I never should have let her bring me back to the community room. I thought that Boost has got to be the most calorie-dense drink known to man. My weight would skyrocket! Plus, if I could drink a Boost they'd wonder why I was even here! They'd send me home for sure, and then I'd never get the help I so desperately needed.

"What flavor would you like?" Sharon asked again.

"I don't think this is a good idea..." I hesitated.

"It's your call," she said.

"Uh...vanilla...?" I finally decided. Okay, I would do this! I was so afraid of having another heart arrhythmia. Each time I had an arrhythmia I worried I would die on the spot – a real possibility. Earlier in the evening I called a therapist I'd worked with when I was younger. I told her that Renfrew was not forcing me to eat on my first day and I asked her what to do. She told me that it was my choice whether or not to eat tonight. She said one night wouldn't hurt anything. I didn't believe her. One night *can* hurt. One night *has* hurt! The truth is, I probably would have been okay either way, but my fear of heart trouble caused me to choose the Boost.

Once I finally decided I would drink the Boost I tried to set aside all excuses. It was excruciatingly difficult. I felt too fat, too weak, and too lazy. I worried about what others would think if they saw me drinking a Boost. I wanted to express my fears and worries to Sharon but I didn't know how. So I cried. Hard. So hard that I got dizzy and fell over. When I finally collected myself enough to continue, I sat down at the table with Sharon and the cup of Boost. Finally I was able to drink the boost. It tasted good, which frightened me. I was scared that if I liked any food I would keep eating and never be able to stop myself. I drank the Boost slowly, a little at a time. I would guess the whole ordeal took about an hour. When it was over and I finished the Boost, I went back to my room, exhausted.

Shortly afterward I was crying again. Once the fear of heart trouble had passed I felt like I had betrayed myself by drinking the Boost. How could I give up all that I had worked for – my diet – the one thing I had going for me? Restriction gave me a sense of control. It gave me a sense of organization and stability, of power and strength. How could I give that up? Why did I give in so easily?

In addition to my sorrow over the Boost, a nurse had accidentally shown me my weight after I had not known it for nearly two months. It was a much higher number than I remembered and I was extremely distraught.

Sharon found me, once again, sobbing on the floor. I was crying so hard my vision had gone speckled. I was dizzy and exhausted. Sharon helped me into my bed.

"But I have to get in pajamas!" I cried.

"You can sleep in your clothes," she said reassuringly, "Girls do it here all the time."

I didn't like that answer and after she left and I calmed down a little bit, changed into pajamas and got back into bed. I had a splitting headache from crying so hard for so long. I was sad. I was angry. I was worn-out and frustrated.

But from somewhere a small flicker of hope had appeared.

2

Week Two:
Accept Your Feelings

Accepting your feelings is the first step in learning to cope with them. Often it is easier to deny your feelings or numb out through self-destructive means such as engaging in eating disorder symptoms. Sometimes you may convince yourself that you are experiencing a "safer" emotion – one that you know how to handle – only to find that your true feelings surface in unhealthy ways. For example, you may be more willing to accept anger than sadness. Anger is often a secondary emotion.

How to

Beware of "cop-out feelings." Bored. Tired. Fat. Sick. These are ways to escape your real emotions and to avoid dealing with them. Recognize your true feelings. Rather than hiding your emotions from yourself, experience them. Remember that feelings are just feelings and although some may seem unpleasant, they cannot harm you. Learning to feel is part of learning to truly live.

When to use this skill

When you experience difficult emotions.

I had definitely gotten across the point that I needed significant help. Perhaps not in the most direct of ways, but it sufficed. Nevertheless, the next day did not prove to be much easier. I struggled through my meals and I cried at every provocation, no matter how trivial. My eating disorder rendered me unable to deal with the every-day stresses of life. I began to wonder if coming to Renfrew was just a big mistake. Eating was definitely not any easier here. I was relieved that my family and I were not fighting with each other over my eating disorder anymore, but it seemed that nothing was improving. I was impatient. It was already the second day! Why didn't I see any change?

I don't remember the precipitating incident, but some-time before lunch I was throwing a tantrum in my room, once again crying on the floor next to my bed. Someone called for Brenda, my therapist. She entered my room and tried to calm me. She asked me to get up off the floor and come to lunch. I was miserable and desperate for some-one to understand. I looked up at Brenda. She looked very young. She had dyed her hair red and wore a nose ring. *This* was my *therapist*? She looked like a high school student! How was I going to work with someone like this, I thought judgmentally?

I glared at Brenda, hoping she would look in my eyes and see the great hurt within. I hoped she could somehow see what I needed and how to support me. Sadly, I didn't think she understood. In truth, how could she? I hadn't said a word to her! But I didn't have the skills yet to understand.

Brenda asked me to get up again. I was so frustrated and angry, and I grabbed a pen and began twisting and bending it against my hand until it snapped. Brenda took it from me and told me that what I was doing constituted self-harm and that if I couldn't keep myself safe then I couldn't remain at Renfrew.

"Fine! Then I'm leaving!" I shouted. I got up and stormed out the door, down the hallway and into the phone booth. Brenda stormed out after me. I called my mother. Brenda threw open the door of the phone booth and ordered me to get out.

"I'm on the phone!" I snapped at her. And not in the most respectful of ways, either.

"You can't be on the phone now. You have to go to lunch!" she countered. I continued to yell into the phone, crying and shouting about how this was all a big mistake and about how I hated Renfrew. I was so upset and I thought that therapy wasn't going to work out after all. How could I work with *Brenda*? She was so *frustrating*! And any chance of a good working relationship was sure to be ruined after this!

"Get off the phone," Brenda warned again.

When I didn't get off the phone, Brenda went down to the team center, got on the other line, called my mother, and told her to hang up on me. Then she came back and told me to go to lunch. This is how I remember meeting my therapist.

My first group that day was the "healing garden circle of life ritual." A basket was passed around and those of us who were in our first week at Renfrew were to close our eyes and choose a rock from the basket. The rocks each had a word painted onto them. We were to then go around the room and say what the word on our rocks meant to us. Each patient was to keep the rock she chose for the duration of her stay at Renfrew. At that time she had the option of taking it home, passing it on to another Renfrew resident, or leaving it in the healing garden.

When the basket was passed to me I closed my eyes and chose a rock that said "try" on it. I thought for a moment and then, not wanting to say something tacky or stupid, I said, "I don't know... I guess it means I have to try to recover." I would later come to find deeper meaning in my "try rock," which I kept, from that day forward, on my night table to remind me always to try.

I met with Jackie that afternoon. Her office had bookshelves filled with nutrition books and pretend food. There was a window looking out onto the front patio where people ate meals outside. Jackie sat in a big, black swivel chair at a desk which held her computer and papers. Next to the desk, near the door, was another chair. This is where I sat. Jackie would soon become one of my favorite people, but she wasn't *that* day.

"It took you *how* long to fill out a menu for one meal?" she asked me. She didn't sound pleased.

Uh oh...

"Trish informed me that it took you *forty-five* minutes to plan dinner?" she said. "For the time being I am going to pick out your food for you."

"No!" I cried. This was *bad*. How could I trust this woman to pick out *my* food for me? She wouldn't have a clue what I liked or didn't like. She'd probably give me the highest calorie foods and think nothing of it! I glared at Jackie and began to cry. What else?

Soon the meeting deteriorated into yet another cry-fest. I was incoherent and unsure of how to express myself. I cried and argued and fought. I made little or no sense, and I knew it, but I didn't know what else to say or do.

"You aren't the girl I talked to on the phone," Jackie chided. Jackie had called my house before I left for Renfrew in order to discuss my keeping kosher. I had been fairly good-natured then, although I distinctly remember warning her that I could be difficult at times, especially regarding food. Now Jackie warned that I was being disrespectful.

I cried and glared and argued but nothing was changing Jackie's mind. The bottom line: Jackie would choose my meals. I would eat them. If I didn't eat them I would have to drink Boost. It was that simple.

Before we finished the session Jackie paused and gave me a serious look.

"You only get one life," she said kindly, "don't waste it on an eating disorder."

The meeting ended and I turned to leave.

"One life," she repeated.

Over the next few days I struggled to eat anything. I cried at every meal. I didn't finish my food. I slept through my groups. Often I didn't even *go* to the groups. Instead I isolated in my room. The weekend was especially difficult, as all the people I had met – Brenda, Jackie, Andrea, and other staff members – had all gone for the weekend. It seemed I was surrounded by new staff members every five minutes. I blinked and shifts changed. I felt confused and alone. I had meltdowns at every occasion and was difficult to work with. At one point Nina, a psych-tech, had to help me to stop hyperventilating and regulate my breathing.

"Do you want help?" she asked me.

"Y-y-yes..." I sobbed.

"Then breathe in," she coaxed me, demonstrating a regular breathing pattern. I breathed in.

"Now breathe out."

But I was still stuck on "breathe in."

"Breathe out..." She repeated. *"Breathe out!"*

It took a while, but I did finally regulate my breathing and I calmed down significantly. Nina taught me that it is easier to calm down and think clearly once I am breathing regularly.

I spent most of the first weekend alone in my room. I cried a lot. At one point Sharon spoke with me. She said that she didn't believe I wanted to get better. She said I fought every helpful suggestion that came my way. While Sharon was correct about the fighting, she was incorrect about the not wanting to get well. I wanted very much to get well. I had fought hard, in my own way, to come to Renfrew in order to get well. I was extremely insulted at the insinuation that I didn't want recovery. I went back to my room and cried. Again. Soon I calmed down enough to write, the only appropriate method I knew of expressing myself. I opened my journal, a brand new striped book given to me by my aunt when I was in the hospital. I began to write.

> I need help. I don't know how to manage my feelings. I don't know how to "sit with my feelings" – especially the hard ones. I find it intolerable and have to "do something about it." I have urges to self-harm in order to neutralize my feelings. I need to learn to tolerate my feelings.

I remembered staff telling me over and over that medication could help me achieve this goal and I added: "I don't want meds." I continued writing on and on. It was cathartic and calming. I wrote down my thoughts and feelings about treatment: "I'm so overwhelmed. I have so much to work on and I don't even know where to begin [or] what to work on first... there's so much..."

I reflected on my meeting with Jackie: "Jackie said I was disrespectful...[I] wanted her to forgive me but I was too embarrassed to ask."

I wrote down some of my worries and some of the things that stood in my way:

> I'm emotionally needy... Many times I isolate when I most need help because I'm embarrassed to ask for help... I worry that crying too much will make me depressed... I have a huge problem with all or nothing thinking... I can't stand others being angry with me or disliking me for any reason... I'm ashamed of all feelings I think are inappropriate... I'm embarrassed that I need too much attention, space, food, money... I'm uncomfortable following rules because I feel like rules are for people you don't trust... I feel like I don't deserve to be comfortable or take care of my body or be happy or have nice things. That's why I've been sleeping on the floor instead of in bed...

I wrote and I wrote and I wrote. When I finished writing I went to sleep, physically exhausted and emotionally drained. I was thankful when the weekend ended and the structure of the week returned.

I met with Brenda on Monday morning. Her office was right next door to Jackie's office. Brenda sat in a big armchair across from a couch, where I sat. The room had a desk next to the door, upon which were Brenda's computer and papers. Above it were pictures and photographs. The room seemed to be decorated in a fish motif, with mementos of the sea scattered throughout – a big stuffed fish signed by a few of Brenda's other patients, an orange goldfish, an origami fish in a bowl, and a fake aquarium.

Brenda introduced herself again and explained that I would see her three times a week for individual therapy and once a week for family therapy which we would conduct over the phone, as my family lived in Cleveland, Ohio. Brenda told me that my current behavior was unacceptable and that if I was to continue at the rate I was going, I could have my level bumped down to day room. I told Brenda that I was very interested in therapy and that I was willing to work hard. I had been in therapy in the past and made immense progress. I learned about myself and I made lasting changes. I was hopeful that therapy at Renfrew could help me and I very badly wanted that chance.

"We will not be doing any therapy until you are completing one hundred percent of your meals," she said firmly. Brenda found her leverage. I glared and argued and cried but Brenda didn't budge. I wanted to do therapy and she was going to use that as a means to get me to eat.

It worked.

Although I struggled and cried, I did eat my next meal, lunch, in its entirety. And I discovered that eating when I was emotional did not turn me into an "emotional eater," one of my greatest fears. It also was not "giving in" or "backing down." In fact, it got me what I wanted – the chance to do therapy and beat this thing for good! I actually felt *better* once I completed the meal.

In the after-meal support group that afternoon, when everyone shared about their meal and the thoughts and feelings that arose during it, I shared that I'd finally realized that none of my issues had anything to do with the food. I said that I just need to let it all go during the meals and eat, because the real issues need to be dealt with in therapy, not at mealtimes. I knew that it was all easier said than done, but at least it was a start.

Although I made progress during lunch, I was still struggling with an overall feeling of confusion and I still felt overwhelmed by all the new information and people I was meeting at Renfrew. Jackie set up a "mini team meeting," a meeting that included Brenda, Jackie, Joy the red team leader, and me. My mom was also included, over the phone. The goal of the meeting was to help me better adjust to life at Renfrew and explain to me who my support people were and how to reach them. I was also warned again that my current behavior may result in my level being lowered to partial, or even full, day room.

We met in Joy's office which was down the hall from Brenda's and Jackie's offices. Joy sat at her desk by the phone, Brenda and Jackie sat on a couch, and I sat on a chair facing them all. We discussed my fear of being lost in the shuffle at Renfrew. I was told that Brenda and Jackie would be there for me and that I could request to see them whenever I wanted. I may not always get a quick response if they were busy, but I could always leave them a message and they would get back to me. In addition, I could call upon any of the staff members for support when needed. At the end of the meeting I felt much better. I was grateful toward Jackie for setting it up.

Later that day I wrote in my journal: "Jackie is the first person here I think I'm really starting to trust. Maybe not completely, but it's a start. She seems sincere. I think she cares. She definitely got things rolling in the right direction today and for that I am thankful."

Although the mini team meeting was helpful and I made progress towards my recovery, the following day was still challenging. In the early morning I was about to have another meltdown. Instead I remembered that I had support people I could count on and I went directly to the team center before I lost control. I spoke with Adam, a practicum student. He tried to help me calm down but my tension level was high and it wasn't working. Just then Jackie came down the hall and helped me pull it together. I already thought highly of Jackie for setting up the mini team meeting and for her patience and concern. I wanted to show her that I could pull myself together and manage. When I felt calm enough I attended my next group. It was a group called "coping with anxiety." How appropriate!

The group aimed to teach the residents of Renfrew to deal with their anxiety in healthy, productive ways. I was by no means the only one at Renfrew to struggle with crying spells and meltdowns. In addition to the emotional baggage each resident brings with her into treatment, a residential eating disorder treatment facility is a very challenging place to be. Coping with one's pre-existing anxiety and depression in the face of finding oneself an inpatient presents a unique challenge.

By the time I went to the following group, art therapy, my anxiety was getting to me once again. The art room was in a different building so I walked there. It was down the front walkway, left, around another building, and up the stairs. It took me a while to find the place, as it was my first time going to art therapy. I was a little bit late and by the time I arrived everyone had already begun to work.

"What am I supposed to be doing?" I asked no one in particular. When I didn't receive an answer I asked again, and once more no one responded. Feeling lost and frustrated, I angrily left the art room, stormed down the stairs and around the building. On my way back to the residence building I felt weak and dizzy. I was so frustrated and anxious and I didn't mind the distraction. I let myself fall. I scraped my hand and my knee. Immediately afterwards I realized that this would not lead to good things, but it was too late.

I remembered my mini team meeting. I remembered how just an hour ago I'd wanted to prove to Jackie that I could handle this. I decided that right now – this very moment

– I would pull it together. I went to nursing to clean up my wounds. I saw Jackie in the hallway again and I made myself relax. I was determined to do this. When I was all cleaned up I went back to art. It was the first time that I left a group and managed to get it together enough to *return* to group. Even if just for the last five minutes, which unfortunately in art therapy is "clean up time."

Since it was a Tuesday, it was time for red team rounds. During red team rounds each patient on the red team individually meets with the red team staff to discuss her progress. Levels are re-evaluated and changes in status, including the privilege of using sharp items at a set time, can be made. Every patient on the red team gathered in the main hallway to await her turn. It was at this time that Andrea, the psychiatric nurse practitioner, called me into her office.

"I really feel that you would benefit from medication," she told me.

We went through this over and over again in our last meeting and several times since. I did not want medication! Or did I? What *really* was the point in resisting at this stage in the game? Was my life really manageable the way it was? I thought about my week – the meltdowns, the crying spells, the falling down, the urges to self-harm – I couldn't risk falling back into a self-harming pattern of behavior. I did enough of that as a young teenager and I knew the horrible feelings of isolation and despair it brought about. The longer I went on like this, depressed and miserable, the more likely I was to succumb to the self-harm urges. I couldn't let that happen. The truth was that over the last few days I was seriously considering taking her up on the offer of medication. I knew that I needed help. However, I was so afraid to take medication again. And it felt like if I was to agree to take medicine again it would reflect badly on me. I had just weaned myself off my antidepressants. How could I admit that I still needed them? I fired my questions at Andrea:

"What medication are you recommending?"

"What dose?"

"How long will I be on it?"

"Are you sure this is the right move?"

"What are the possible side effects?"

"What if I change my mind?"

And I *did* change my mind. Several times. During that one meeting alone I went back and forth over and over again. I wanted to give myself every advantage in my recovery, but I wanted to stay true to my reasons for not taking psychoactive medication.

I was first prescribed antidepressants at age fourteen during a bout of depression and anorexia. I wanted it then, as I thought medication was the magical quick-fix. I soon found it was not. It caused side effects and it took some adjustments before any positive effects were evident.

Around the time I was preparing to graduate high school, I spoke with my psychiatrist about weaning off the medication. I wanted to live on my own and I felt that the medication was a crutch. I wanted to live independent of medication, just as I assumed most others did. We worked out a plan to slowly decrease the amount of medicine I took. I went to study in Israel, and continued to decrease my medication even without a psychiatrist's supervision. I so badly wanted to come off the antidepressants. I didn't want to rely on something external to help me regulate my moods. It felt shameful. I should be self-sufficient. I thought that goal was inconsistent with taking medication.

Furthermore, as I sunk deeper into a depressive state, I became convinced that my new depressed, obsessive thoughts made me a deeper, more mature person. I wasn't fluffy and fickle like other people my age. I was dark and brooding. I thought deep thoughts and contemplated serious issues. No one understood me, but I didn't *want* to be understood if it meant being shallow.

Nevertheless, I knew I couldn't continue at the rate I was going. I couldn't risk falling back into self-harming habits. Through previous therapy I came to recognize self-harm as a way to distract myself from dealing with real issues. It was a pseudo solution that caused even bigger problems. And it was very difficult to discontinue. I also feared that if I didn't try the medication, my insurance might stop paying for treatment since they'd see I wasn't complying with Andrea's recommendations. I agreed to hear her out.

Andrea patiently explained that the medicine, an antidepressant, would help stabilize my mood so that my "lows" would not be quite so low. Once my mood was more stable, I would be better able to do work in therapy. The medicine would help me do the work. It would not do the work *for* me. My progress and recovery would still be in my hands. After all, if medicine was the magical quick-fix, there would be no need for therapy at all. After listening to her proposal I realized that I owed it to myself to have every advantage in my recovery. The medicine would make it easier for me to learn new coping skills and do work in therapy. I would keep those skills even after I discontinued the medicine. After nearly an hour of back-and-forth talking and reasoning and discussion, I finally and tearfully made the incredibly painful decision to go back on medication. It was a major step in the right direction.

Unfortunately while I was making that decision, my team was taking steps in another direction and decided to put me on full day room. I was fuming. Here I was making the excruciatingly painful decision to do what was best for myself and go back on medicine, and they were deciding to drop me *two levels*!

My team was concerned for my safety and well-being. They felt I needed additional structure and support, as well as continuous supervision. Until now I was skipping groups, leaving groups and going to my room where I would listen to depressing songs and sleep. I wasn't interacting with the other patients and I was throwing temper tantrums and meltdowns multiple times a day. My team felt that full day room would provide me with the support necessary to overcome these behavioral issues.

On full day room I would have to spend all my time from 8:00 am to 9:30 pm in the community room, which is also known as the "day room." I would continue to eat all of my meals in the day room. I could only attend groups that met in the day room and if I ever had to leave the day room, for instance to use the bathroom, I would have to be escorted by a staff member. I would be watched every minute of every day. It wasn't fair! And, of course, right after I received this news it was time to go to lunch. How perfect. But I remembered my goal to do therapy and I did get through the meal.

I met with Brenda later that day. She explained to me that they decided that full day room would be the best thing for me right now. On full day room I would not be able to isolate in my room. I would be forced to interact with the other patients, something I had not done as of yet, and I would have the opportunity to form relationships with them. Brenda felt that full day room, though unpleasant, would help me progress in my recovery. I heatedly disagreed. Brenda also suggested that I purchase silly putty to help me relieve anxiety.

In the beginning I was sorely tempted to "prove" to Brenda and the others on my treatment team that full day room was the wrong choice. I wanted to do everything in my power to show them that it would only make things worse. I wanted to have even more meltdowns and show them that just because I could not be in my room didn't mean I would magically develop friendships with the other patients. I also felt that there was no point in trying to improve anymore since I was already on the lowest level.

But then the more mature part of me kicked in and I remembered that I came to Renfrew to heal, not to be stubborn and get my way. I was also afraid that acting out might result in Brenda revoking my therapy privileges again, like she did when I wasn't eating. I went to the Renfrew store and bought silly putty, which I came to rely on quite a bit. I told myself that day room would only last for one week. Next Tuesday I would earn level one back again. Even though the rule seemed to be that no one could move up two levels in one week, I felt confident that I would be the exception. I still felt superior to the rules and decided to humor them only for my own benefit.

I was sure I would hate it, but I soon found that full day room was not as terrible as I originally thought. I met many girls and although I was still pretty self-absorbed I listened in on several conversations. I was astounded to hear of the serious medical consequences some of the girls experienced. And some of them didn't even seem to mind!

"I have osteoporosis now," said Melanie to a group of women in casual conversation one day. "My doctor said he'd never seen a worse-looking spine in a sixteen year old."

No one seemed shocked. Each woman in the group had experienced her own medical consequences. But I could sense in many of them that they still felt in some way it was worth it in order to continue with their eating disorders. I was beginning to realize that this is a very scary illness.

Before I left Israel I confided in a friend that I had an eating disorder and that it was the reason I was going home early. Because I had been very ill before I went home, my friend knew that something was wrong.

"Oh thank God it's just an eating disorder!" she exclaimed, "I thought it was something serious!"

"Yeah," I responded. "Thank God." And I meant it.

For me to now recognize the seriousness of an eating disorder was a huge step forward.

Later that evening I met with Cara, a practicum student working with Brenda. My session with her was productive. We discussed my need to overcome the fear of my own feelings.

I had discussed with Brenda and written down several factors that kept me from functioning. At the top of my list was emotional neediness. I felt dependent on others for emotional support, for attention, approval, and security. I depended on others in order to feel safe enough to venture out in life.

Fear was another factor. I was afraid to feel like "just another..." I was afraid of being average and forgotten. I was afraid to try my hardest in case my hardest wasn't good enough. I often would not try my hardest because of this fear, preferring instead to maintain the belief that if I *had* given it my best, I would have been a brilliant success.

Other factors standing in my way were my insecurity, the degree to which I was judgmental, subject to guilt, impatience, exhaustion, discouragement, anxiety, perfectionism, thinking too far ahead, and overanalyzing every situation. There were so many factors and so many feelings involved. But Cara was right: I was afraid of my own feelings. It was far easier to believe that I was "just sad."

Until now I had been turning every feeling into "sadness" and then reacting to it as if it was indeed sadness. I cried over everything. But it never solved anything because it was a response to an imaginary problem. My goal for the following day was to do what I needed to do and go where I needed to go and to feel whatever feelings arose and not to hide from them. It would be challenging but I felt confident that I could do it by remembering how badly I wanted recovery. Cara encouraged me.

"Vulnerability leads to strength," she said.

3

Week Three:
Use Your Voice

When you use your voice you communicate what you think, feel, and need in a healthy and appropriate way. Others can understand you and the lines of communication are opened.

How to

You may wish to act out your messages – consciously or unconsciously – with your body, through drama or other attention-seeking behaviors in the hopes that someone will understand, only to be disappointed when they do not. Instead, put words to what you need. Voice your hurt. Take a deep breath and confide in someone you trust. Explain verbally what you need and how you can be supported. When you speak, others can listen.

When to use this skill

When you need to communicate and be understood.

*O*ver the next week I practiced feeling my true feelings and not running from them. It was difficult and I struggled with meltdowns and crying spells. Another Renfrew resident told me during a therapy group to "turn stumbling blocks into stepping stones." I appreciated the analogy and I tried to use my struggles to my advantage. I told myself that they would make me stronger. I still struggled through groups and meals, although I continued to eat one hundred percent. I tried to follow the rules of full day room, but between escorts and phone times, group schedules and meals, there just seemed to be so many of them. When I broke a rule, however, I was upfront about it and made sure to inform Brenda. On Thursday I attended my first "inspiration celebration," a patient-run spirituality group composed of readings, stories, and music. I had my first family therapy session that Friday and it went well. Despite my concerns that my parents and I had already gotten as much out of family therapy as possible in previous years, my parents showed willingness to explore our relationship further and to better it in any and every way possible. They wanted me to recover and were willing to do anything in their power to help. The week progressed and while I was never thrilled about being on full day room, I saw the light at the end of the tunnel when team rounds rolled around the following Tuesday.

Before each week's team rounds, every patient fills out a form saying a few words about her recovery in various categories such as emotional stability, psychiatric concerns, and nutritional goals. There is also a section where one may request a level change, or other change in status. I requested three things. I wanted to move back up to level one, I wanted to get off sharps-restriction so I could use my sharp items, and I wanted to eat breakfast in the dining room. I was nervous but hoped for the best. I felt I had good reasons for requesting these changes in status. For instance, level one would give me the opportunity to prove that I could participate in groups and interact with other patients instead of isolating, even when I was not forced to do so by my level. Surely my team would see my progress in such a short period of time and let me have the few things I asked for.

Since I had missed what was supposed to be my first team rounds the week before, when I met with Andrea about the medicine, this was an introductory meeting. Rounds were held in the community room and I was shocked by how many people were in the room. Brenda, Jackie, and Joy were there. So were Andrea and a few nurses I recognized. The other therapists and psychiatrists and staff members on the red team were there as well.

I sat down in a chair at the front of the room. Everyone on the red team staff went around and introduced themselves to me. Then Brenda explained that since I made progress this week they were going to move me to partial day room, one level up. Before I went into rounds a girl named Danielle on the red team had warned me not to get my hopes up, that the treatment team would decide what was best for me, but that I may not get everything or anything I asked for. I asked for three things. My team was very sensitive and tactful in explaining that they felt I was not yet ready for the privileges I requested and I was surprisingly okay with getting only half of one of them, in part due to the kind approach of my team and in part thanks to Danielle's warning. Danielle had been at Renfrew a few weeks prior to my arrival and was at this point farther along in her recovery than I was in mine. She was strong and spirited and I looked up to her.

Danielle grew up in a military family and moved around a lot during her childhood, something that was often difficult for her. She developed anorexia following a traumatic event at age ten. Her secrecy kept her from achieving recovery and at age fourteen she was admitted to a residential eating disorder clinic. Not ready to recover and still very secretive, she played the system and even picked up new eating-disordered behaviors.

After her discharge from the clinic she underwent further treatment for her eating disorder and for a suicide attempt, eventually leading her to maintain a healthy weight, although not a healthy mindset, throughout her high school years. After high school there was a lot of uncertainty in Danielle's life. Her future held a lot of unknowns. She felt comforted by what she *did* know – anorexia.

She relapsed in college and was admitted to the Renfrew Center following her sophomore year after her therapist gave her an ultimatum: either she would undergo treatment at Renfrew or her therapist would stop seeing her.

After her first stay at Renfrew, Danielle maintained recovery for a year and a half, at which point she relapsed again. This time it was Danielle who sought treatment for herself. As she put it, she used to have a "road map" of when certain effects of a relapse would occur and when she would lose healthy functioning. This time she became very ill very fast. She was scared and didn't want to die.

She admitted herself to Renfrew once again. She knew she couldn't do this to herself anymore. She was so tired of being sick. She missed being happy. She wanted to truly live her life. This time would be different. Upon her latest admission to Renfrew she met with Jackie.

"I won't do this anymore," Danielle said, "I can't go back."

"But you *can*," Jackie answered, "What if you do?"

Together Danielle and Jackie worked through a description of what would happen if Danielle chose to relapse again.

"It is a choice, Danielle," said Jackie.

The conversation hit home for Danielle, who could no longer say even to herself that this time would be different without a commitment to actions that would *make* it different. Danielle, like everyone at Renfrew, had her struggles and challenges. Some she shared with others and some were hers alone. I knew very little of her story as I stood with her in the hallway that day, but already I admired her for what I did know.

Danielle was a couple years older than me and seemed so put together and confident. I'd seen her around Renfrew but until now I rarely spoke with her as I was a bit intimidated. She gave off a sense of courage and confidence. She spoke her mind and stood up for herself when something bothered her. She even called me out during a community meeting and explained to me that my meltdowns were affecting the entire community and needed to stop.

I had tried to ease up on the meltdowns and I think this helped Brenda and the red team staff members make their decision. On partial day room I still had to be in the community room from 8:00 am to 9:30 pm, but I was allowed to attend groups outside of the day room as long as I was accompanied by a staff member. I still had to have escorts to and from various places, including the bathroom, but I was allowed to eat in the dining room. That is, if my nutritionist, Jackie, let me. She did not. But I was okay with that. I knew I wasn't ready. I still used far too many food rituals and I still wasn't working on any of them.

My treatment team also felt that I would benefit from doing a "stage one." The stage one was a contract between my treatment team and me that required me to seek support from the Renfrew residential community during the next community meeting. I was to specify the inappropriate behaviors I was struggling with – having meltdowns and throwing temper tantrums – and explain how I was going to do things differently. I was to ask for support from the community, telling the other patients what they could do to support me, and I would receive feedback from my peers. A goal of the stage one was to aid me in learning to communicate my needs verbally, rather than through meltdowns and crying spells. It was to take place on Friday morning.

I had a full week. I still cried and struggled at meals, I had several more meltdowns, but I worked hard in therapy, slowly learning to vocalize my concerns, and each meltdown was shorter and less intense than the last. The medicine seemed to be kicking in and I adjusted better to life at Renfrew. I felt somewhat less depressed. A number of significant events occurred that week.

On Thursday I had my very first Meal Support Therapy (MST) group. MST is a lunch group in which therapists eat lunch with their patients and process any concerns or problems that arise during the course of the meal. My group was led by Brenda, and I ate lunch with her and all of her other patients living at Renfrew.

Throughout the meal Brenda and the other girls engaged in pleasant conversation. Brenda began a casual discussion and from there the conversation drifted onto other topics smoothly and comfortingly. The conversation did not revolve around food or body image. For the first time since I arrived, I felt part of a group of women, not merely eating disorder patients. I mostly just listened as the others talked, but I appreciated the discussion very much. It was the most normal mealtime conversation I'd experienced in a very long time.

The meal went smoothly enough. It was my first time eating outside of the day room and I felt nervous and anxious. I was extremely self-conscious and wasn't at all sure I would be able to complete my meal. I had only recently begun to work on reducing my use of food rituals. My first food ritual reduction assignment from Jackie was to "keep my fats where they belong." For example, no more peanut butter on pizza. Peanut butter contained lipid nutrition, and as a food group was considered a "fat." I was to keep it where it belonged, meaning in a sandwich with jelly, or on apple slices or crackers. Putting it on pizza was inappropriate, considered to be a food ritual and not allowed.

I was beginning to heal my body through proper nutrition and I naturally had a better sense of which foods went well together but it was still difficult to break old habits. I finally opened up more with Jackie and she helped me find ways to work on reducing my food rituals at my own pace.

With consistent proper nutrition it was becoming easier to eat in a more normalized way. I recently discovered the very first food combination I did not like – bananas and ranch dressing. It was such a novel discovery that there actually existed an unpleasant combination of foods, that I celebrated my normalcy that afternoon.

Despite my self-consciousness and my anxiety, MST went well. Another significant milestone of the week was that for one of the first times, *I* asked for a contact, rather than having staff run after me trying to calm me down during a meltdown. I went to the team center and asked for Denise, a kind counselor I had come to trust over the past couple of weeks. We discussed a few ways to combat anxiety and to feel more "in the moment." In particular we reviewed mindfulness skills – being fully aware of my surroundings, using all of my senses to experience my environment, and being more aware of myself. I felt significantly more relaxed when our contact ended.

Later that week I was feeling anxious and a bit stir-crazy in the day room. I got into an argument with Denise over the phone times for day room patients. I had confused the times and used the phone when I was not supposed to be using it. The mistake was quickly rectified and I resumed using the phone at the appropriate time. Unfortunately another patient had seen me earlier and thought I had been on the phone for a lot longer than I had been. She told Denise who asked me to get off the phone. I tried explaining to Denise that I was not on the phone for a very long time, but she insisted that I get off anyway. I blew up at Denise, yelling at her that she didn't trust me so why should I trust her! Later that night I felt bad and apologized to Denise for my inappropriate behavior.

The following day was extremely stressful for me. I did my stage one a few days earlier and was assigned another one that morning, as my meltdowns had not yet ceased to occur. In particular they wanted me to mention the phone incident which led to my yelling at Denise. I was told during team rounds that I would not be moving to level one just yet – but that they would re-evaluate my level on Friday after my second stage one.

I was frustrated and requested a mini team meeting. I had frustrations regarding my progress in therapy and regarding my weight and nutritional goals. I was frustrated that I did not get level one for the second week in a row and I tried to show Brenda, Jackie, and Joy that I was ready. They still did not give me level one. During the meeting I found that I could not seem to communicate effectively through the spoken word and I felt discouraged and angry. Despite my hard feelings, I did what I had to do and went to the 5:00 pm group after the meeting, although I truthfully did not participate much.

Soon it was time for dinner and I was beyond overwhelmed. I asked Krista, the psych-tech with whom I had been eating dinner quite often, if I could sit farther away than usual because I was struggling and needed space. But before we could reach a compromise on where I would sit, I noticed that there was less food on my tray than my menu indicated there should be. Jackie my nutritionist wanted me to start eating more snacks. But how could I, I thought, when it wasn't even okay for me to have my whole dinner? Although the kitchen had simply made a mistake, I took it personally and internalized the message that someone must think I was too heavy, otherwise they would have given me all of my food! I asked Krista if I could go find Jackie or some other nutritionist to ask about dinner. Krista said no. She said to just sit down and eat. I felt powerless and anxious and never wanted to eat again. I doubted if I would ever recover from my eating disorder and I stormed out of the community room and knocked on the team center door where I was told that all the therapists and nutritionists had gone home for the evening. A nurse told me that it was in my best interest to go back to the community room and eat dinner. But by then I was too worked up.

The previous week I had met with Jackie, who told me that you can't "half" get rid of an eating disorder. You either keep an eating disorder or you leave it completely. Until this point I was doing so well with eating one hundred percent of my meals that I thought I was completely recovered. If my eating was "all better" and I could still restrict the way I was doing now, how could I ever know if I was truly recovered?

I was so overwhelmed, not knowing whether to trust anyone, and if so – who? I cried and I cried. I decided not to have a contact or talk to anyone until I had calmed down. I was very upset and didn't want to end up overreacting and saying something I would regret later, the way I had the night before with Denise. I was trying to avoid a full meltdown. In that moment, I felt that restricting was the only option. I would not eat dinner and everything would somehow be okay soon. It was just one time. How bad could it be?

Soon Krista came and tried to get me to go back to dinner. I didn't want to go and I didn't want to talk. I wanted to sleep and escape from the whole thing. I kept trying to make Krista go away. I wanted to sleep. Who knew? Maybe when I woke up I would feel differently about food again. Dinner time soon ended and an after-meal process group was underway.

Just then another patient came to the team center with a massive nosebleed and needed to go to the hospital. Krista told me that I had to leave the area, as the emergency medical service would arrive soon. She asked me to go into the community room, where the process group was taking place. I refused, telling her that processing my current situation would get ugly. I told her that I didn't want to say or do things I would regret later.

Soon it was too late for that. Krista kept insisting that I go to the community room. I kept refusing. Finally I felt completely overwhelmed and trapped. As we walked towards the community room, feelings of overwhelming anxiety welled up in me and I got this sudden rush of having to *do* something. There was little thought involved at this point, just emotion. I felt trapped and sequestered. I had to get out. I shouted, "I'm leaving!" and "I'm going home!" over and over. I ran into my room and threw my things into a suitcase, crying hysterically and thinking to myself, "oh no! What am I *doing*?!" I knew I couldn't leave. But I felt like all hope was lost, that I'd really crossed the line this time and there was no going back. I didn't know how I would ever live this down, at least in the immediate future. My actions that night were just another way of *showing* that I needed help when I couldn't manage to outright *ask* for support.

I frantically packed up my things and headed for the door. It was not a well-organized escape plan. I had forgotten all of my belongings that were on shelves higher than eye-level and I had somehow lost my shoes. So essentially I was attempting to run away with no shoes and no money. Krista and two nurses came into my room and tried to calm me down. I wanted to scream out, "I'm so sorry! Please help me fix this!" But I just kept crying and not making a lot of sense when I spoke. They left the room and I cried very hard. Then I calmed down a little bit and decided that I would take responsibility and ask for what I needed. Verbally.

I walked down to the team center and knocked on the door. Angie, a counselor, answered.

"I need help," I told her. It was not easy and it was a monumental step in my recovery. Angie took me outside to talk. We walked out to the patio outside the dining room where people ate their meals. We sat down and just as we began to talk, someone ran outside with a cell phone.

"It's Brenda!" she called.

I spoke with Brenda on the phone for only a few minutes but it was a crucial conversation. I told Brenda what had happened that night. I told her that even though I was acting out, all I really wanted was help. I finally expressed *verbally* that I needed help! I worried that there was no way that I would get level one on Friday after this. Brenda told me not to worry about Friday and just to deal with tonight. I told her I was so sorry for making such a big mess. Brenda accepted my apology and assured me that it was all fixable and that *I* could fix it. When we hung up I felt confident that I could make amends and grow from the experience.

After the phone call I apologized to all the staff involved, including one poor psych-tech who had just begun to work at Renfrew (at least I gave her a memorable first day!) and I went to the dining room with Angie to have dinner. Then Krista helped me unpack my belongings and put my room back in working order. (I can only imagine what my new roommate was thinking!) When I was done I wrote a letter to my team. I explained what had happened and why I did what I did. I explained what I learned that night – that attention-seeking behaviors such as having meltdowns or trying to run away were not providing me with the kind of attention I was actually seeking. The only attention that felt good that night was the attention I received after verbalizing my needs and asking for support. I realized at last that no one can read my mind. That glaring at people, trying to communicate through my eyes, does not help people understand me. Meltdowns do not resolve any issues. "I need help" – in those three words I accomplished more for my recovery than I had in the preceding *month* of meltdowns. I also learned that I am not perfect but that I can always fix things, and that using my voice is the skill that facilitates the fixing.

It was a difficult night but it was a turning point. The night I attempted to run away was my last and final meltdown.

That Friday was a big day for me. I had two stage ones, family therapy, and my medicine was being changed. Brenda promised me for days that she would be there for me. But when Friday finally rolled around, Brenda called in sick. I felt disappointed, angry, and abandoned. I was counting on her to be there to coach me through the day and she wasn't coming.

At first I was angry at Brenda, feeling like I had trusted her and she let me down. I thought angrily that she'd better be really sick if she wasn't here with me. But then I caught myself and realized that Brenda hadn't let me down before and that she probably had a good reason for being out today. I felt bad wishing her ill.

I complained to a bunch of people, didn't want to eat breakfast, and didn't want to do my stage ones. But then I realized that this would be the perfect opportunity to prove that I could handle anxiety and depend a little more on myself, rather than on the Renfrew staff, to help me manage my feelings. I was determined not to meltdown or mess up.

After breakfast I met with Joy, the red team leader, instead of Brenda, to discuss my stage ones. I voiced my feelings and concerns to Joy. She told me that Brenda was really sick but that she had still wanted to come in today to be there for me. She told me that Brenda realized that today was an important day for me and she felt bad missing it. She also explained that Brenda made arrangements for me to be taken care of in her absence: Joy would meet with me about the stage ones, Joy would lead my family therapy session, and the rest of the red team would re-evaluate my level that afternoon.

The morning went well. I ate breakfast and did my stage ones, which were quite entertaining. People seemed amused by my story about trying to run away without money or shoes. The medicine change was very stressful but I made it through.

At the end of the day I achieved level one.

4

Week Four: Be Creative

Journaling and art are two ways to explore your thoughts and feelings through creative expression. They can help you put things on paper (or on a canvas or in clay) and out of your mind. This can help you gain insight and understanding as well as a new perspective. When you express your thoughts and feelings this way, you no longer have to carry them around in your mind and heart. Art therapy is an especially good way to explore and express things that are not easily put into words. You can learn a lot about yourself by looking back over your creative endeavors and examining your thought patterns.

How to

Don't worry about perfection. Just write, paint, sculpt, sing, whatever. How do you best express yourself? Use your talents to help you in your recovery.

When to use this skill

When you have strong feelings or thoughts that you want to explore or process. When you can't talk with someone. When you want to remember something. When you have circular thoughts that you need to end.

I was moving ahead in my recovery and was making progress every day. But I still found it painful to be gaining weight and I was often dissatisfied with my changing body. I began to romanticize my eating disorder and wish that I could lose weight once again.

I came to therapy sessions with my journal, and both Brenda and I realized that writing was a strength of mine in recovery. Brenda began to teach me new ways to use my writing talent. To combat my unhealthy thoughts about my eating disorder, Brenda had me write out a list of what my eating disorder had cost me. After careful thought this is some of what I wrote: **Therapy assignment: what my eating disorder cost me**

- It cost me my ability to think, focus, remember, and reason well.

- It cost me my ability to thermoregulate – my body's ability to regulate its temperature within normal limits.

- It cost me my ability to just sit down – I had to carefully position myself because my body felt like a bag of fragile crystal.

- It cost me healthy circulation. I cut off circulation to different parts of my body in most positions. Socks cut off circulation to my feet.

- It cost me my care and belief in most things. I struggled with my religious faith.

- It cost me pleasure in everything. I literally survived hour to hour.

- It cost me trips I would have enjoyed if I was healthy.

- It cost me my period.

- It cost me my ability to walk well and do stairs.

- It cost me my comfort. My body hurt all of the time. I had chest pains and heart arrhythmias.

- It cost me bladder control. I had accidents – and a horrible bladder infection.

- It cost me interest in my future and the energy to want to live, which made it easier to turn to anorexia, the one thing I still had "going for me."

- It cost me my interest to ask questions in school.

- It cost me my commitment. I did only what I had to do to "get by."

- It cost me my social life. I stopped caring how others were doing.

- It cost me my job. I quit my work study job at the gym so I could sleep more.

- It cost me my confidence. I never got to "show off" how thin I got because I was too cold and had to wear several layers of clothing all the time, and because I was self-conscious. I knew people would be horrified if they saw me without so many layers.

- It cost me my health. I had horrible "starving breath." A nutrient deficiency caused my breath to smell horrible. I lost a lot of hair.

- It cost me my hobbies. I stopped writing.

- It cost me my options. I made decisions based on my illness.

After I wrote the list I took it back to Brenda and we reviewed it. She helped me remember how miserable I was when I was living in accordance with the rules and dictates of my eating disorder. She told me to remember how unhappy I had been and what the anorexia had cost me every time I began to think of all the "good" I could get from an eating disorder. She helped me see the "good" for the illusion that it was. She reminded me that I was young and therefore had the great opportunity to leave the eating disorder now before I had more to add to my list, such as missing out on having a career or a family. I felt sad for the older women who came to Renfrew, having lost so much to their eating disorders, and I was determined not to arrive at the same fate. I would beat this thing now.

Journaling was so far my best strategy for healthy self-expression. I learned about myself through journaling and often found that once I expressed things on paper I no longer needed to express them through unhealthy attention-seeking behaviors, such as engaging in drama or eating disorder symptoms. I strengthened my resolve to participate more in my groups at Renfrew and learn even more ways to express myself healthily.

Renfrew provides many opportunities to engage in therapeutic creative expression, such as movement therapy, psychodrama, and art therapy. I participated in all three.

When I attended my first movement therapy session I was unsure of what to expect. I walked into the movement room, which I knew best because it was also where inspiration celebration was held, and joined a fairly large group of women. The room was large and the floor was cleared. There was patient artwork covering the walls and the filing cabinets.

Cecilia, the movement therapist, instructed us to join together and form a large circle. She put on soothing music and joined the circle.

"We will go around the circle several times," she said, "and each of us will make a body movement that the others will copy. I will begin."

Cecilia made a movement and then the woman to her right copied the movement, followed by the woman to *her* right, and so on, until the movement had traveled around the entire circle. Then the woman to Cecilia's right made a different movement that traveled around the circle. It continued this way until each of us had chosen a movement.

"Very nice," said Cecilia. "Now I want each of you to choose your favorite movement." We went around the circle again, this time each of us performing the movement we liked best. I chose Chantal's movement. Chantal was a woman I ate with in the day room. She arrived at Renfrew brain-starved and without a lot of apparent personality. Now she was beginning to open up more and more, through proper self-care and nutrition. Her movement was to hug herself, gently rocking back and forth. Self-love is a significant part of the recovery process. Seeing Chantal give herself a hug somehow impressed upon me the message that even if I found myself all alone, *I* would still be there to love and take care of myself.

When we had each chosen our favorite movement, we broke into two groups. Cecilia had us each take with us the movement we chose and incorporate it into an interpretative dance that would tell a story. At first my group didn't know where to start. Then I took charge, for possibly the first time since I'd been at Renfrew. I had each of us review our movements with each other and then I had an idea.

"This can be the story of how a person learns to trust," I said. I demonstrated through the movements. I began with a pacing movement chosen by another woman. "At first we are not sure who to trust." I made Chantal's movement. "Then we must learn to trust ourselves..."

"Then we can hesitantly reach out to another," added another woman in the group, making a reaching movement and quickly withdrawing her hand.

"Yes!" I said.

"And then..." Other women began to chime in with their own ideas. We incorporated each of the movements into the dance and told the story of the struggle to learn to trust.

After the two groups had finished, we exchanged dances and stories. Cecilia liked our work and even asked my group to perform our dance for the entire Renfrew community during this week's inspiration celebration. We agreed.

I walked out of the movement therapy room that day amazed at what had taken place. We had expressed, as a group, the challenges posed by the desire to trust. Many women in the room had traumatic experiences in their pasts, some having been betrayed by those closest to them. Through movement therapy, we were all able to come together to express the pain of broken trust, as well as the hope and resilience that would lead each of us to trust again. And in doing so, we had trusted each other. Movement therapy seemed so unconventional to me at the start of the group. I hadn't known what to expect or how it could possibly help. But it taught me a new method of expression, as well as a way to join with others in my treatment at Renfrew. It showed me that I was not alone, that my struggles were shared by others. And right now that was exactly what I needed.

Feeling less alone, I volunteered to participate in psychodrama. I sat nervously in my seat in the community room before group started, because I knew I would be volunteering today and I knew it would be a challenge. The group was led by a man named Claude, a talented group leader, who worked off the information his participants provided him and engaged us in role play. During a psychodrama session, the patient spoke with Claude as if he was someone else. The patient chose who Claude would pretend to be. Sometimes he was a patient's parent. Sometimes he was a patient's friend, sibling, eating disorder, or higher power. He could be anyone or anything a patient requested. The conversations he then had with the patient would encourage skills such as conflict resolution, integrity, assertiveness, and truthful expression. I nervously awaited my turn.

Claude entered the community room and took his seat at the front of the room. I raised my hand and he called on me.

"I would like to go today," I said.

"Who am I going to be?" he asked me.

"My father," I told him.

I told Claude a little bit about my relationship with my father and then we began the session. My goal was to finally express in words, to Claude as my father, the truth about what happened in Israel. I was so ashamed that I'd needed so much help and guidance during my first year in Israel and I feared that if I told my father the truth he wouldn't be proud of me anymore. I felt it was a terrible secret. As if I was supposed to be perfect and never need support from anyone.

"What would you like to tell me?" asked Claude, acting as my father. It was difficult at first, but I kept reminding myself this was important. I needed to get this out. Holding it inside me, along with all my shame and fear, wasn't healthy.

"I want to tell you the truth about my first year in Israel," I said.

"I'm listening," said Claude.

I began by telling him about my motives to make him proud of me. How I'd tried to master the third movement of Moonlight Sonata on the piano and how I'd wanted to come home better in all ways, so that he would be proud of me. I spoke about aspects of our relationship about which I usually remained silent. And finally, I spoke the truth about my relationship with one of the principals of my seminary. I took a deep breath.

"He helped me so much. I was not as independent in my accomplishments as I led you to believe. I met with him every Thursday morning. He guided me through the year.

He watched out for my safety, and he came through for me more times than I can even tell you. At one point he even set me up with an on-campus therapist! I was afraid to tell you this because I wanted you to believe I was strong and independent and didn't need that kind of help anymore."

Claude responded by telling me that my accomplishments were still mine and that he was still proud of me. When the role play ended, I got feedback from the other women in the room. No one thought it was as dark and horrible a secret as I had feared. I was encouraged and told that everyone needs support. And I realized that they were right. Just speaking it out loud and having the discussion helped me realize that this wasn't so terrible. It was actually quite normal. I realized that sometimes when I hold things inside they seem huge and terrible, and when I express them in a healthy way they often feel less scary.

After psychodrama that day I went to Brenda and requested extra phone time. That night I called my parents. I had the same conversation that I'd had in psychodrama with them, only this time it was real. I was relieved to hear the same encouragement from my father that I had received in group.

Psychodrama proved to be great practice for the real thing on several occasions. And sometimes, like the time I asked Claude to be my eating disorder, I learned more about myself through creative expression. It was a wonderful tool in my recovery.

Art therapy was also an important part of my treatment at the Renfrew Center. Although my first trip to the art room had left much to be desired, my later sessions were extremely productive. They became a wonderful expressive outlet for my thoughts and feelings about what I was going through. They taught me about myself and allowed me to be freer in my self-expression.

One assignment was to create an image of my eating disorder. Upon hearing the task at hand I knew immediately what I wanted to do. I sat down at the table and for a moment I was lost in a memory...

When my health had begun to deteriorate in Israel I was in deep denial. But one night as I was falling asleep a black and white image of a dirty old rag doll being strangled in a kitchen popped into my head. The doll was freakishly thin and had a possessed and miserable smile plastered onto its face. Its eyes were blank and dead. The word "anorexia" flashed through my mind as I jolted awake.

Now in the art room at Renfrew I remembered the feelings of fear and entrapment the dream had triggered in me. I was determined to capture those feelings in a work of art. I asked Kim the art therapist for charcoal and I drew, to the best of my ability, the image that appeared in my head that night in Israel. When I was finished I had another idea.

I tore up the picture I just created. Then I carefully pieced it back together on another sheet of paper, deliberately leaving white spaces in between each of the torn pieces. When Kim asked me what the picture was about I told her first that the image of the strangled rag doll represented my eating disorder. I told her that I was no longer following the rules and dictates of my anorexia and therefore I tore up the picture. But the hold the eating disorder had on me was not entirely gone – I could still make out the "rules" I was "supposed" to be following. So I pieced the picture back together. The white spaces in between the pieces represented my new life after anorexia. It was white, to represent newness and a fresh start. But it did not have a definite form yet. At the moment all it served to do was separate the pieces of my anorexia more and more as time went on. Kim liked my explanation and I felt good.

Another art project was an unstructured painting. Being a perfectionist, I never felt "worthy" of an art canvas. I thought I would just mess it up, so why should I have one? But one day I decided that if I was going to get over my perfectionism I should just ask for a canvas and start painting. So I did. Kim gave me my first canvas and I colored all over it using watercolor pencils and water.

At first it looked like a jumbled mess and I wanted to give up and consider it a mission failed. It had a shooting star here, a bunny there, a coconut tree on an island in a third place. Random pictures facing random directions were everywhere! The painting made no sense. But I persevered and stuck with it and kept painting and coloring and when I was finished, a few art sessions later, it looked wonderful. It was a collage of color. I called it my "random color explosion" and felt very good about it. I had finally gone with the flow a little bit and given up on perfection. It was okay to make mistakes. Some of the mistakes were the best parts of the painting! I was determined to carry this life lesson from the art room out into the rest of my life.

Another assignment was to paint a mask.

"Your assignment is to paint a mask," said Kim the art therapist, handing me a plain white mask. "Paint a representation of what you show the world on the outside of the mask," she instructed. "And on the inside of the mask show what you truly are. When you are finished, please write up an explanation for your work."

I took the mask and I thought for a while. Then I had an idea. On the outside of my mask I painted a regular human face with blue eyes and dark blond hair. No makeup, no frills. I even dabbed on a little reddish paint to show some zits. When I finished painting most of the outside of my mask, group was over. I was disappointed.

The next time art therapy came along I was excited to have a project to work on. Over the next few sessions I continued working on my mask. On the inside of my mask I scribbled with oil pastels in many colors. I taped colorful construction paper to the inside and glued in chunks of colorful tissue paper. I splattered paint over it all, again in many different colors. Kim walked over to me and commended me on my work. She said it was very interesting and asked to hear my explanation. After she had read what I'd written, she asked me to share it with the rest of the group. I read aloud:

The front of my mask is a regular human face. No makeup or add-ons or anything. I usually present myself that way so that is how I painted my mask. I don't like wearing makeup because I feel like I have something foreign on my face. I also don't like not being able to touch my face. It's the same reason I don't like wearing fancy clothing very often. I don't want to worry about ruining them. I want to just live.

The inside of my mask is a collage of colors – all different textures, paints, oil pastels, paper, and tissue paper. It represents all of what makes up who I am. All of my talents and interests. Everything I have to work with. There is a lot. Not to be conceited but I'm very intelligent, have many talents and interests, and really do have a lot inside of me. Unfortunately it is all over the place right now and very messy. I feel like at Renfrew I am cleaning my garage, in a sense. First I have to take everything out, figure it all out, and then put it back in the right place. It always looks messier before it gets cleaner. Right now I am in the messy stage. But it's okay because I'm making progress and I am getting myself together. Also I'm only twenty years old and I don't have to know everything now. I don't have to have myself all figured out immediately.

One thing that stuck out for me as I did this project was that the random colors all over the place, while messy, were fun and exciting! It is okay to go with the flow a little bit, like I did in this project. My life can be fun and exciting and livable without having every detail all planned out. I'm going to be okay. I *am* okay.

The other girls in the room applauded my work and I sat back down at my table. I reflected on the project I had just completed. I had been to a few art sessions by now. I never imagined I could learn so much about myself through art. There was so much I could express through art that was difficult to put into words. This surprised me. Throughout my entire life, my primary form of self-expression and self-exploration had always been writing. From the time I was a little girl of five I had been keeping notebooks and journals. It was new and exciting to now discover other methods of self-expression and exploration.

Soon Jackie decided, along with the rest of my team, that because I was doing so well at keeping away from food rituals, I was ready for the next step in the meal levels – eating in the dining room.

The first of the meal levels is eating in the day room on trays. "Trays" refers to the fact that one's meals are approved by one's nutritionist, prepared ahead of time and brought out on a tray during mealtime. The second level is eating in the dining room on trays. On trays the patient must have her food checked before the start of the meal to make sure everything is as it should be, and at the end of the meal her trash must be inspected to ensure that all food was consumed. The third meal level is called independent eating – IE – and this is when the patient goes through the line and chooses her own food, but must have everything inspected and signed off by a counselor or psych-tech before beginning the meal. Trash is still inspected. The fourth level is called fix-owns and that is where the patient not only chooses her own food but is also trusted to complete her meal in its entirety without being checked up on. Tables in the dining room correspond to the different meal levels. Patients on fix-owns have the privilege of eating outdoors.

I was nowhere near ready for this kind of independence, but I was now deemed ready to move from eating my meals in the day room to eating in the dining room. It was a momentous occasion. At first I was very frightened and self-conscious that my food, being kosher, was different from everyone else's food. I thought that people would stare at my food and ask me why it was different. But that did not happen. For the most part everyone kept to the rule that stated "keep your eyes on your own tray." I was grateful. I adjusted to eating in the dining room quite nicely.

Another exciting event was my medical clearance for exercise. I was now able to participate in exercise A, which was held twice a week. During exercise A we learned to be conscious of our bodies' needs and messages. We walked, skipped, and stretched. After attending two sessions of exercise A, I was eligible for exercise B, during which we were also allowed to run, jump rope, and play catch.

By this point even I knew I was making significant progress in my recovery. I was no longer obsessing over food, I was physically able to participate in gentle exercise, and I had long since stopped my constant comparing myself to other eating disorder patients. I had also begun to think outside of myself, often telling others that if they wanted to talk I would be there to listen. This was something I couldn't have begun to imagine doing when I was critically ill. I had begun to overcome my food-related shame by having open and honest conversations about it with Jackie. My mind was clearing up. I was able to read again. I could hold intelligent conversations. Food really was medicine!

Doing well, I was soon moved to level two. On level two I was allowed to go out in the sun and use the pool. On Sundays I was able to get a massage. The new privileges felt very rewarding.

Despite the fact that I was doing well in most aspects of my recovery, I still lacked adequate self-esteem, an issue that is by no means unique to eating disorder patients. To help combat my low self-image Brenda had me write out three lists. On the first list I was to write "I am" followed by all the negative words I thought about myself. The second list was to be identical to the first, except that instead of writing "I am" I was to write "I am not." The third list was to be a list of new positive "I am" statements. My finished assignment looked something like this:

I am	I am not	I am
big, fat, unlovable, ugly, incapable, miserable, pathetic, lazy, sick, crazy, delusional, insignificant, stupid, fake, worthless, disturbed, clumsy, average, fragile, immature, embarrassing, shameful, guilty, fickle, insecure, draining, boring, cliché, sappy, annoying	big, fat, unlovable, ugly, incapable, miserable, pathetic, lazy, sick, crazy, delusional, insignificant, stupid, fake, worthless, disturbed, clumsy, average, fragile, immature, embarrassing, shameful, guilty, fickle, insecure, draining, boring, cliché, sappy, annoying	lovable, intelligent, creative, unique, pretty, capable, friendly, sincere, important, deserving, worthy, healing, real, honest, strong, flexible, special, helpful, valuable, healthy, talented, funny, loved, happy, alive, lively, energetic, secure, optimistic, enjoyable, worth it, good, understanding and understandable, trustworthy, dependable, determined

When I finished writing Brenda had me read my lists aloud to her during an individual therapy session. Although it was surprisingly difficult, it did seem to help me feel better about myself. For starters I realized that many of my negative self-beliefs were based on thoughts that did not make sense. How could I consider myself *fat* when every doctor and nutritionist I had seen wanted me to *gain* weight? How could I consider myself *unlovable* when my family was behind me and supported my treatment one hundred percent? I was certainly not *incapable* – look how far I had come already! After completing the assignment and discussing it with Brenda I felt significantly better about myself. She told me to refer to the list whenever I was feeling down.

Deciding to tackle other issues with Brenda, I completed many more assignments on topics such as anger, cognitive distortions, and family history. Each brought about new self-awareness and emotional stability. One of the most significant assignments I completed was called a "thought record." Brenda taught me about counter journaling through the thought record.

The thought record was designed to combat cognitive distortions such as catastrophizing – thinking the worst will happen, generalizing – assuming that all similar situations will end with the same results, and all-or-nothing thinking. By correcting these cognitive distortions I would improve my thinking and my mood.

For each distressing situation I was to record the precipitating incident, my automatic thoughts and feelings, evidence that supported my thoughts, evidence that didn't support my thoughts, a new, balanced way of looking at the situation, and my mood after completing the exercise.

While completing this assignment I was surprised to discover that the reasons I was so easily upset were rooted in my erroneous thinking patterns. For example I was very upset upon hearing that Danielle had been to Renfrew twice.

But when I recorded my thoughts I realized that they were misguided.

My initial reaction to hearing that she had been to Renfrew twice was to respond in jealousy and discouragement. My automatic thoughts were that Danielle must be more special to Renfrew since she had pre-existing connections with the staff. I thought that once isn't enough and that I would have to come back to Renfrew a second time as well. I felt jealous and wanted to come back a second time myself. Evidence that supported my thoughts was that many girls who had come to Renfrew twice seemed to know the ropes and have deeper relationships with staff. Evidence that didn't support my thoughts was that many of the girls who came to Renfrew for a second time were very sick and somewhat less hopeful that they would really recover. Why would I want to feel that way?

My new balanced thoughts were that the girls who had been here twice certainly had some advantages but they had some disadvantages as well. I am not in a contest with anyone and there is no basis for comparison. It is best for me to focus on myself and on my own recovery. I need to make this my first and last stay at Renfrew – to get well and stay well. In the end I was calmer, more peaceful, and less jealous. I also felt sorry for the girls who had been here twice because it meant that they had struggled for a long, long time.

I continued keeping the thought record for a while until the process became so second nature that I could think it through in my mind without the need to write it down.

At my next meeting with Brenda we discussed the number of contacts I'd been having. Brenda assured me that it was a good thing for me to be seeking help when it was needed but that perhaps I was going overboard. She advised me to consider ways in which I could self-soothe and handle my feelings without staff support. We brainstormed ideas together which included journaling, talking to my friends, and doing art work. We also discussed the real reason that I sought contacts. It boiled down to attention. I was now to work on giving *myself* attention and getting attention from *friends*, and therefore needing less attention from staff.

That night I met with one of the counselors and told her what I discussed with Brenda. I told her the real reasons I went for so many contacts with staff members. I told her the plans I thought out with Brenda. The counselor encouraged me to be more self-reliant and to reach out to other girls in the Renfrew community when I felt the need for attention. I knew I could do it. Already I was seeing changes in myself. Many people speak of a metaphoric "eating disorder voice," which tells them to engage in eating-disordered behaviors. I now listened to what I came to call my "Renfrew voice," which told me to be strong and that I did not need to feel triggered. It told me I only had one life and to use it well. My Renfrew voice sounded a lot like Jackie!

I strengthened my resolve to become more self-reliant and not to need constant attention and care from staff. I continued to reach out to others in the community, offering my support to them. I wrote letters and drew pictures for other patients, trying to bring them a spark of happiness and to show them that they were not alone.

Overall I was becoming more even tempered and patient. On the morning of June 26, I was running late because I overslept, which resulted in my inability to participate in the exercise group. I was surprisingly okay with that. Others expressed to me that they had been worried about how I would react and that it spoke to my hard work and commitment to recovery that I'd remained composed and calm through-out the confusion. By now it was becoming second nature to remain calm under pressure. I was learning that all the panic and anxiety in the world doesn't change any given situation. It was much easier to deal with conflicts when calm. It was also far better to live and make mistakes and learn from them than to try to stuff life into a tiny, confined box and try to be perfect. I had come a long way.

In an afternoon group that day I realized just how *far* I had come. The topic of the group was body image. Angie, the counselor leading the group, taught us a new form of creative expression. The day's assignment was to write a letter from our bodies to ourselves. We weren't given much thinking time. We were asked to just write the letter on the spot. I wrote:

Dear Naomi: I am so glad you are feeling better now. These past several months have been really hard on both of us. I'm so happy you started eating again and are learning to appreciate all the important things we need from food.

I want you to know that I am not, and never was, angry with you. Even during the darkest times when you weren't feeding me, I did not reject or resent you. If I had we never would have survived. I used every bit of energy I had to keep you alive and functioning to the best of your ability under the circumstances. I lowered heart rate and metabolism to conserve energy to afford you survival – to ensure that you would have the chance to heal someday. I'm so glad that you are. I'm glad also that what you once perceived as my weakness, you now recognize as strength.

As for body image, I understand that you are dissat-isfied with various parts of me and often with my gener-al appearance. I hope in time you will come to see health as beauty. We are very lucky to have found help when we did. Because of that I was able to recuperate and heal you completely physically and enable you to work through your mental and emotional pain.

We are going to be together for a long time. I'm so happy you're learning to love me as much as I love you. I am a gift from God to be cherished and cared for. Always remember that [the purpose of] my whole existence is to better your life. I am endlessly devoted to you. Love, your body.

When we were done writing, the group instructor asked for volunteers to read their letters aloud. I volunteered and read my letter to the group. I got amazing feedback.

"You must be very far along in your recovery if you are able to write a letter like that!" one girl commented.

"Yes," agreed another girl, "I wish I was doing so well!" Many others in the group expressed similar sentiments.

I sat back and took it all in. For the past few months I had sat in groups and listened to girls who had been at Renfrew for some time talk about their recoveries. Listening to them gave me hope that someday I would overcome my strong eating disorder urges. I listened to the girls who had been there longer than me in awe, wishing I could someday be the girl others looked to for inspiration, and that someday I too would be far along in my recovery. It seemed that moment was now. It didn't happen overnight by any means. It took hard work and painstaking effort. But during moments like this one it all felt worthwhile. I sat back and smiled.

5

Week Five: Reach Out to Others

Reaching out to others involves both caring for others and letting others care for you. Healthy relationships require both kinds of reaching out.

How to

Reach out to others when you need support as well as when they need support. Do something to help another person. It doesn't need to be anything huge. A simple smile can brighten another person's day. Show your care and appreciation with a kind word or a special gift. Listen to what others have to say and let them listen to you. Notice what is going on in the lives of those around you. Offer support. Accept support.

When to use this skill

When you are building and maintaining relationships. When you are with people. To keep yourself from isolating.

*T*hrough creative expression I was learning to trust myself more and more each day. I could reliably figure out what I was feeling and then find ways to express it to staff members when appropriate. I was doing well, yet something was missing. I felt too isolated. I was healing but I was lonely. I saw many women around me at Renfrew. They talked and spent time together outside of group therapy, doing puzzles, playing games, and watching movies. They seemed so close to each other and I longed for close friendships as well.

I worked with Brenda to determine a specific goal – to reach out to Danielle. I had known her for a while now and I thought we could be friends if I would only learn to overcome my reluctance to, and fears of, befriending my peers.

It was an issue that went way back to my earliest years when, even as a child, I preferred to sit and talk to my preschool teachers at recess rather than play with the other children. I worried they would tease me or make cruel jokes, which I was certain adults would not do. I remember my mother saying that I would be a happier adult than child because I seemed to get along better with those older than myself.

But as I grew older I remained uneasy about relationships with my peers, preferring instead to associate with those in positions of authority. I felt safer talking to bus drivers than passengers, parents than siblings, and teachers than students. And now at Renfrew I felt safer with treatment professionals than patients. How could other patients support me when they themselves had the same problems? And how could I, in turn, support them?

I also feared closeness with others because I didn't want to hear anything I would have to keep secret. This stemmed from an experience I'd had when I was ten years old at a going-away party for my best friend Cassie from school who was moving far away. Cassie had a vivid imagination and was somewhat troubled. She told me she had a secret – that she could tell the future. She began making terrible predictions, explicitly warning me of tragedies that would supposedly befall my friends and family and warned that I had better not tell anyone her secret, otherwise she would die. When I told her I couldn't keep silent about such terrible things Cassie responded, "Do you want to go to your best friend's funeral?"

I was petrified and grew weak and dizzy. My parents were called to pick me up from the party and were simply told I was upset because of mean fortune telling. After the party I distanced myself from my friend. I didn't want to hear any more scary secrets. I refused to come to the phone when Cassie called. I avoided her until she finally left town.

Although Cassie's secret was far removed from reality and her predictions never came true, my fear was real and from then on I avoided closeness with others my age, for fear that they might burden me once again with a terrible secret I could not share.

As an adult I realized that the secret was evidence of Cassie's own troubles. I knew that it was harmless to me and that nothing bad had or would happen to my friends and family. I wondered, therefore, why the secret still hindered my ability to become close to others. Brenda helped me understand that I had not received Cassie's secret as an adult, but rather as a child, and therefore I reacted to it as a scared child who believed her friend.

To help me overcome this fear of secrets, Brenda assigned me to more challenging groups, in which I would hear disturbing "secrets" of others, and taught me a sentence that I often repeated to myself when I was afraid: "Their stuff can't hurt me and my stuff can't hurt them." It took some time, but I slowly learned to tolerate hearing private information again. Thus I was able to begin reaching out to others in a deeper and more real way.

"Naomi," Brenda asked me in a therapy session, "Who, of the current Renfrew residents, do you think you can best relate to? Do you admire anyone? Is there anyone you think could be a friend?"

I considered her questions and immediately thought of Danielle. Through our group therapy sessions together I learned some of what she'd been through and I admired her strength. I saw how she related to other people with confidence and self-assurance. She seemed so self-validating and secure. She also sat with me at MST and periodically glanced my way with a supportive look on her face. It was evident that she was working hard in her recovery while at the same time caring for others. I was certain she would be a good influence on me, although I didn't know what I could do for *her*. "I want to be friends with Danielle," I said to Brenda. I expressed my concerns about not having anything to offer in a friendship.

"You have plenty to offer, Naomi," Brenda challenged me. "Think of ways to reach out to Danielle."

After our session I continued thinking of ways to strengthen my friendship with Danielle. I drew upon writing and art to help me. I wrote a letter to Danielle:

Dear Danielle, You may not know it, but you've been a support to me. You give honest and encouraging feedback in groups and you really help me out at MST... I admire how real you are. As far as I can tell you don't play games. You say what you mean and express your truth. I look up to you for that. I'm at a point in my recovery where I'm trying to reach out to others... You've been a good influence and I guess I'm hoping some of your courageous sincerity and confidence will rub off on me. I have a lot of respect for you and wanted you to know that. Sincerely, Naomi.

I folded up the letter and put it in Danielle's mailbox. The following morning as I sat in line waiting to have my vital signs taken, I watched nervously as Danielle, wrapped in a fluffy pink blanket, made her way over to her mailbox and read the letter. I anxiously waited as she read it, wondering how she would respond. She finished the letter and walked over to me.

"Thank you," she said, giving me a hug. I felt good.

The following week I reached out again. After a difficult group in which Danielle had opened up about her struggles and disappointments, she was clearly feeling down. At Renfrew we were taught to have a mental "safe place" to go to when we feel anxious or are dealing with stressful issues. Danielle loved the beach and I knew it was a place where she felt peaceful and content. My next group that day was art therapy and I knew exactly what to do.

I entered the art room and made a beeline for the box of wood. I found a small wooden plaque and took a seat. On the wooden plaque I drew the beach. I colored a palm tree, sand, and the ocean. I made it as beautiful and peaceful as I could. Then I wrote another letter:

> Dear Danielle, You're working so hard and it shows. You're an inspiration to me... I know there probably isn't a lot I can do to help you, but I know you like the beach and you've told me before how good you feel there at sunrise. So during art I wanted to make you a concrete reminder of a "safe place" I know feels good to you. It's a small gesture but I hope you find some comfort in it. I'm thinking of you and wishing you well. Love Naomi.

I took the beach plaque and the letter and handed them to Danielle. I walked away and waited while she read the letter. Minutes later she approached me with tears in her eyes.

"I *love* it!" she cried, "This is so special; this means so much to me!"

Later on Danielle told me that my gift had really helped her. She said it reinforced the work she was doing with Brenda and she was very appreciative. Danielle told me she was working to strengthen her self-confidence. I could hardly believe it! *Danielle*? The one I looked to as a *role model* of self-confidence? She said my letters helped her see positive qualities in herself that she was working to achieve and that it was so good for her to see that they were evident to others.

Over the next several weeks, Danielle and I spoke more and more, eventually becoming close friends and remaining close long after our time at Renfrew.

Another woman I began reaching out to was my suitemate Victoria. (She lived in the room that shared a bathroom with my room.) Victoria was tall and had long, blond hair. She wore bright red lipstick and spoke in a deep, loud enunciated voice trained by years of professional acting. She was passionate and lively and spoke her mind in groups with confidence.

As I rarely did my makeup, and usually kept my long hair tied up to keep cool in the hot Florida summer, it was a big step for me to allow Victoria to do my hair and makeup one morning, something she had offered to do a few times before. We talked and laughed as she curled the bottom of my hair and applied a moderate amount of makeup to my face. I looked in the mirror and smiled. Victoria did a beautiful job. Throughout the day I received compliments from other patients and staff members. Jackie was happily surprised to see me "all dolled up," and commented that I was clearly enjoying myself.

Victoria and I sat together at meals and talked. I told her about my life in college and she told me about her acting career. I had fun trying to imitate the way she spoke, using her "real voice," as she called it.

"Most people don't use their real voices," Victoria explained, "Instead they speak from their throats and their voices come out softer and more strained."

She explained that through her training she learned to speak using her real voice. I was fascinated and tried to use *my* real voice. I didn't have the kind of extensive acting training that Victoria did and I couldn't seem to find my real voice, although I did find my "hoarse old man voice." We laughed.

One night Victoria moved upstairs, a reward for her progress. She moved into an empty room on the second floor. I went to visit her. We spoke for a while and I opened up to her about my fears regarding friendships. She was totally understanding and encouraged me to reach out at my own pace. I looked around the room and realized that Victoria didn't have a roommate.

"What if I moved upstairs?" I wondered aloud.

"That would be so cool!" Victoria said, "We could be roommates!"

We talked about how fun it would be to live in the same room as the time grew late. As I prepared to go downstairs to my room, Victoria stopped me.

"Want to hang out at the pool tomorrow with a bunch of us?" she asked me. I hadn't been invited to many social "events" at Renfrew and it felt so good to be included, to be really joining the community.

"Definitely," I answered.

Over the next couple days I spoke with my treatment team and made plans to move upstairs. We all felt I was ready.

Unfortunately I could not room with Victoria. She had broken a serious Renfrew rule and was made to move downstairs. She was in danger of having to leave Renfrew altogether. I tried talking to her, but it was no use. Her treatment team had dropped her level down to full day room and she was miserable. She sat in the corner of the room and wouldn't talk to anyone. It was as though she had given up on recovery. A short while later she transferred out of Renfrew and we lost touch.

Nevertheless, reaching out to her helped *me*. I showed myself that I was capable of offering support to others as well as receiving support from others. And although I was sad for Victoria, I knew I had done what I could for her and now it was time to accept that I didn't have control over anyone but myself.

I continued reaching out to others, taking greater and greater risks. I befriended Amelia, a newly admitted patient, and allowed myself to become close with her. She opened up to me about her story and I found that I was not afraid.

Amelia could not pinpoint when her eating disorder began. Rather, she felt it had always been a part of her. When she was five years old she was already comparing her body and food intake to that of others. If her friend ate two brownies, she would eat one. She believed from an early age that it was better to be younger, thinner, smaller.

During her teenage years, Amelia internalized a lot of negative thoughts and feelings about her parents' divorce and her breakup with her boyfriend. She found that controlling her eating habits gave her something to focus on other than her family life and whatever else was bothering her. It became a way to cope with difficult events and her feelings about them.

Despite her severely low body weight, slowed thinking and other symptoms, Amelia remained unaware that she had a problem until she was confronted by her mother and a counselor. At that point she was in deep denial, yet began working with a counselor who specialized in eating disorders. She tried to recover as an outpatient but soon found she needed a higher level of care. The structure of Renfrew brought her a sense of relief.

We got to know each other during a break between groups in the day room. I helped her with a crossword puzzle and we discovered that we both enjoyed playing games. We began regularly playing a game called Taboo, making up our own rules and thoroughly enjoying each other's company.

The real game of Taboo is a series of cards and a timer. The first player tries to help the second player guess the word on the top of each card while avoiding the words beneath it. For example, player one may try to help player two guess the word "bed" without saying the words, "sleep," "pillow," or "blanket." They try to match as many words as possible before the timer runs out.

Our version was a bit different.

"I'll say the top word backwards. Try to guess what it is," I said, laughing one day as we sat playing our version of Taboo down the hall from Brenda's office.

"I'm ready," giggled Amelia.

"Serrrgnok!" I burst into laughter.

Eventually Amelia identified the word "congress." Then it was her turn.

"Azzip! Azzip!" she cried.

"Pizza!" I deciphered and we laughed once more.

Amelia and I had bonded.

After nearly two weeks on level two I was making progress and preparing for level three. I even wrote out goals – ways in which I would further challenge myself in my recovery – for level three with Brenda:

1. I will challenge myself to be even more involved in groups.

2. I will challenge myself not only to participate in [group therapy] conversations but to initiate conversations as well.

3. I will challenge myself to buy myself something nice that I will enjoy "just because," and not because I need it.

4. I will challenge myself to become closer to other patients even though we will most likely not keep in touch. (I was afraid of forming attachments and subsequently missing people.)

5. I will challenge myself to speak and act with more self-confidence.

6. I will challenge myself to prepare for discharge and going home.

I was doing well. I had a minor setback at one point but quickly fixed it through effective communication. On Saturday June 30, I had difficulty with a conversation that took place in one of my groups and subsequently struggled through dinner. When staff asked me to complete my meal I was less than cooperative. In a letter to my treatment team I explained my behavior, detailed what a proper course of action would have looked like, and expressed my hope that they would still give me a chance at level three. I included in my letter that my team often taught that "a slip doesn't equal a relapse." I asked them to consider the incident a slip. I told them I was ready for the next level and asked them to let me prove it. That week I got level three.

Level three afforded a whole new set of challenges and opportunities at Renfrew. In addition to weekly massages, the privileges of using the pool and being out in the sun, level three patients engaged in new therapy groups. One group was the supermarket tour, where patients were guided through the process of grocery shopping and taught healthy ways of selecting food. In another group, cinema therapy two, we watched movies that were not allowed to be seen on levels below level three because they were particularly challenging or triggering. In that group we discussed the difficult thoughts and feelings that arose during the course of the viewing. There was a cooking group during which we learned to cook quick and balanced nutritious meals.

There was also a group where the level three and four patients prepared to mentor new incoming residents. Mentoring consisted of giving the new patient a tour, explaining the rules and structure of Renfrew, and answering any questions that the new patient had. I eagerly volunteered.

When my day to mentor any incoming residents arrived, I sat at breakfast watching the front walkway in eager anticipation, watching for possible new patients. I was excited when I saw suitcases being brought to the residence building on a giant cart, because it was evidence of a new patient that I would get to mentor! After breakfast I found the new patient and introduced myself. I asked her to meet me outside the team center after the last group of the day.

That evening I took Aurora on a tour of the building. I showed her the dining room, the different group therapy rooms, the nursing station and I pointed out the other Renfrew buildings in the distance. I answered her questions and tried my best to help her feel at ease. Afterwards I introduced her to other women I knew in the community. It went smoothly and was a typical mentor meeting.

Soon I moved on from my first carefully planned and somewhat awkward interactions, and my reaching out to others became more fluid and natural. I began initiating conversations to support others and in doing so I strengthened my own sense of competence and well-being.

One night, for instance, as I sat upstairs on a bench beneath the hallway skylight looking up at the stars through the window, I noticed Sierra, a fifteen-year-old patient, repeatedly pacing the hallway. Sierra was a girl who constantly gave advice during group therapy, but fought her own recovery. She had some issues with her family and was fighting her parents by hurting herself. She'd been in and out of treatment many times in many centers, and this wouldn't be her last residential stay.

I asked her if she wanted to talk and she said no. I said "sit down" and patted the seat next to me. She sat and we talked. Mostly I listened. Sierra told me that she was not speaking to her parents because that is how she's "fighting." She thought that by talking to her parents she would be communicating the message that everything was okay when in truth it was not. She told me that she just wanted to be a normal kid and not bounce in and out of treatment centers anymore. Sierra said she was thankful she was only fifteen years old and still had her whole life in front of her. In the end she gave me a hug and told me that she felt better. In truth I probably felt even better than she did. I was able to support other people and it felt amazing! Someday I really would use my experience to help others.

The following day during an art therapy group, I caught a glimpse of myself in the mirror. In major contrast to my usual reaction, I was comforted by my own image much the way I was comforted by seeing Brenda or Jackie. I immediately connected it to my supporting others. Interacting with and supporting others was changing the way I viewed myself. I was strong and capable and I was going to make it.

6
Week Six: Relinquish Control

Being open to new experiences can bring about unanticipated gratification and progress. Opening up to others about your struggles leads to understanding and compassion. It is okay not to have every step of your life planned out. It is okay to re-evaluate and change course. Life is full of constant changes and developments. Welcoming those changes enriches your life.

How to

Be open and try new things. Relinquish some control and go with the flow. If an old plan no longer fits, let it go. Open up to others you trust when something is bothering you. You don't need to hold your pain inside. You are not alone.

When to use this skill

When trying new things or asking for support. When planning your future.

*D*uring a milestone MST group, Brenda and her patients gathered around two green tables on the patio with their lunches. I had been to a few of these groups by now and felt increasingly more comfortable at each one. I was more at ease when I ate and I even joined in the conversation. By now I was familiar with Brenda's other patients and I enjoyed their company.

Today Danielle and a few others were teasing Brenda about the pretend fish in her office. They seemed to have a running joke concerning fish and I didn't understand why. Someone else spoke first.

"What's with the fish?" one woman asked.

To answer, Brenda told a story that strongly and positively impacted the way I viewed change and the way I went about planning my future.

"I didn't originally plan to be a therapist," Brenda said. I looked up, surprised. Brenda went on to tell her story.

As a little girl growing up in Connecticut, Brenda was always playing in streams. Her favorite animal was the manatee and she loved everything to do with the ocean. As she grew older she aspired to be a marine biologist so she could, among other things, train animals at Sea World. She moved to Florida to attend a college with a strong marine biology program.

During her senior year she landed an internship at an aquarium. But as she worked there Brenda's heart went out to the dolphins in captivity without vegetation and away from their natural habitat. She also realized that with a career in marine biology she wouldn't have very much flexibility in regard to where she could live.

During the course of her studies, Brenda had taken a number of psychology electives. She loved them and excelled in them and in her senior year of college Brenda changed course and decided to pursue a graduate degree in mental health counseling.

"I originally planned to train sea animals," Brenda concluded her story, "but then I decided to train people instead."

I was in awe.

Until now I had assumed that to be successful in life I had to have every step all carefully planned. Beginning in the tenth grade I mapped out my future with lists and charts. Once I decided, still in high school, to pursue study in psychology, I planned every step leading all the way to my doctorate. And of course I *had* to get a doctorate. It was the best, the most, the highest degree possible and I had to have it.

And so, with my limited eighteen-year-old knowledge, I set off on a course of action to eventually obtain my Ph.D. It never occurred to me that I could change course or even that there existed other options to consider within the field of psychology.

And here, sitting across from me, was Brenda – Brenda, who had her heart set on becoming a marine biologist. Brenda, who I greatly admired. Brenda, who had the openness to change and grow, to allow herself new experiences. And to thrive.

I knew that Brenda loved her work. She loved doing therapy and told me that she had "followed her passion" in becoming a therapist. I thought about the fish in Brenda's office and what they represented. Brenda was a therapist, but she had also been, at one time, a student of marine biology. When Brenda changed career goals she did not turn her back on her interest in marine biology, rather she embraced it as a part of herself. Today, she was a therapist living in Florida with fish in her office who no doubt still loved the sea. It was not her original plan and yet she was happy and fulfilled.

I realized then that the same could hold true for me. Why should I lock myself into a set course of action just because I "made up my mind" in high school? Was that even what I still wanted? I loved psychology, but the feeling of obligation to my "plan" was wearing on me. So many things had changed already – I had moved back home, I had transferred to a new school, I was an inpatient at a treatment center! None of those things were in my "plan."

And yet I was okay. The world didn't end. To the contrary, I had this incredible opportunity to learn and grow at Renfrew and to apply my lessons learned, not only to my immediate recovery but to my life as a whole.

It was still possible, even probable, that I would continue my studies at the doctoral level, but for the first time I was open to the possibility that I did not *need* a Ph.D. in psychology and it was a huge relief. And it occurred to me that if I could change my academic priorities and goals, I could change other parts of my life as well. There were many areas of life that could be much more pleasant if I was open to new experiences and change. I was inspired.

On July 4, Independence Day, Renfrew was in celebratory spirits. One of the staff members decorated his car in red, white, and blue and parked on the lawn. We had a barbeque for lunch in the decorated dining room. Each patient was given a small American flag as a souvenir. Staff really put effort into making it a nice day and it was very enjoyable.

We also had a special Independence Day therapy group which was to last over an hour. Until this point I had trouble staying focused and present during such long groups. Instead my mind would wander to questions such as "what's for lunch?" or "am I getting fat?" or "when is this group going to end?" So needless to say it was a challenge for me to attend such a long group.

I played with my silly putty, which although I originally bought to please Brenda had come to aid me in concentration and focus, and I paid attention to the group leader as she explained the assignment.

She spoke about independence and what it meant to each of us. She handed out "declarations of independence" and asked us to fill them out, declaring independence from our eating disorders for a specific amount of time. The aim was to set reasonable and attainable goals that we could easily reach and thereby boost our confidence in overcoming our eating disorders for good.

After we filled out the forms we each took turns reading them aloud to the entire group. I declared independence from body checking and looking in the mirror for ten hours. Other girls declared independence from behaviors such as ordering only "safe" food at meals, comparing themselves to others, and obsessing over their "sick clothes" (clothing that fit them when they were very ill).

At the end of the group we had a surprise song and dance. It was really fun! I thought about how I had wanted to leave the group several times because of its overwhelming length. I began to cry, thinking that I would have missed this if I left. I thought of all the progress I had made at Renfrew once I developed the openness to try new things. I cried (happy tears) thinking of all the new experiences I would have now that I was emotionally stable once more. Life can be so much richer than I let it be up until this point. I learned to relinquish some control and to my surprise it was not terrifying. In fact it was gratifying. This was a beautiful moment.

July 5 proved to be a much more stressful day. My family went on vacation to Colonial Williamsburg and since I was still in residential treatment at Renfrew, they left without me. I was feeling left out and far away, although truthfully I was extremely glad to still be in treatment. I knew that I still needed to do more work before I went home.

That night a girl at my table was struggling and she binged and purged. I had a hard time dealing with it. I did not want to act out on my symptoms but it triggered many eating disorder urges in me and I subsequently wrote a letter to Jackie detailing my worry and anxiety triggered by the incident.

The following day I met with Jackie in her office. We went over the letter I had written to her the night before and I had the cry of a lifetime.

"Jackie," I sobbed, "I never want to eat again!" I was so scared of liking food too much, of overeating, and of my weight continuing to climb. I was so afraid of relapsing when I went home.

"Naomi," Jackie said ignoring my irrational eating disorder talk, "your fears of leaving Renfrew and of going home are driving the loudness of your eating disorder right now."

"You really think so?" I asked.

"I *know* so," said Jackie. "You should journal about this."

"I don't want to eat!" I cried again, not sure what else to say but trying to drive the point home. I did not see how journaling would help me want to eat again.

"Naomi, I am not going to beg you," Jackie said. "Ultimately it is your choice whether or not to restrict. I don't do cheerleading. What I can do is remind you that you only get one life. If you choose to restrict again it will lead you down the same path you have already traveled. You will be throwing away all of your hard work and progress. You will be missing out on your life." I sat silent for a moment and Jackie continued. "Naomi, when I first met you I thought to myself, 'I don't know *how* I'm going to work with this woman!' You were all *over* the place! You have done a total one eighty and changed so much for the better. I'm so proud of you, Naomi, and I'm here for you."

Jackie was so supportive. I cried, letting out all of my sadness and frustration. I told Jackie my fears of going home. I told her my fears of never amounting to anything. I told her I was afraid I would miss her and Brenda and the others I had come to trust and respect here at Renfrew. Jackie sat with me in her office for a long time, supporting and encouraging me – but not "cheerleading." She stuck with the facts. What was encouraging to me was the fact that she was right – I had come such a long way and I truly *had* made a lot of progress. My hard work and effort was paying off and I was seeing results. Why would I want to throw that all away?

I calmed down and prepared to go on with the rest of my day. Jackie told me again that she was proud of me and that she was there for me. I had needed Jackie that day and she had been there for me. She seemed to genuinely care. I walked out of her office determined to make my "one life" count.

7

Week Seven:
Be Your True Self

An eating disorder can be a quick identity. You may feel it distinguishes you and makes you special. You may fear giving it up because you fear losing a part of yourself. Developing a healthy identity will aid you in your recovery and help you live a healthy, meaningful, and fulfilling life.

How to

Remember that your eating disorder is a conglomeration of maladaptive coping skills. To recover, you need not relinquish a part of yourself. Rather, you retain your full identity as you channel the energy that went into your eating disorder into healthy coping strategies. Accept yourself for who you truly are, independent of weight and body image. You are special and unique without your eating disorder. Have the courage to believe in yourself.

When to use this skill

Always.

*a*n important level three group was the Saturday excursion where a group of patients went out into the "real world" with a counselor and participated in everyday activities that often posed a challenge to someone struggling with an eating disorder, such as clothing shopping, or eating popcorn at the movies. It is crucial for women struggling with eating disorders to learn to participate in a wide variety of "normal" activities.

My first excursion was to the mall on Saturday July 7. At 1:00 pm a group of girls on levels three and four went on an outing to the mall with Krista the psych-tech. The assignment was to try on at least one top and one bottom. We would also eat an optional snack outside of Renfrew.

First we all took off our name tags and went down to the team center to sign out. Then we headed out to the parking lot. Danielle and another girl were driving. At first I got into Danielle's car, but as soon as we pulled out of the parking lot, every other girl in the car pulled out a cigarette. I don't smoke and I felt very uncomfortable. I sat there, frantically thinking of options. *I can try to ignore it... I can try not to breathe a lot... I can say something... I can get out of the car... If I leave, what will the other girls think? What if they think I'm being a baby? What if they find it offensive? What if they don't like me anymore?* But I finally decided that I needed to first and foremost protect my health. That's what I came to Renfrew for in the first place, isn't it? I asked Danielle to pull over and I got out and rode to the mall in the other car. I tried not to worry about what the girls in Danielle's car must be thinking or talking about. When we got to the mall Danielle came over to me. It seems I had no reason to worry at all.

"I'm really proud of you for taking care of yourself," she said. "That took strength."

Our first stop at the mall was to Old Navy. I walked into the store and felt immediately uncomfortable and out of place. For religious reasons it was weird to be out on a Saturday. All the other girls seemed so comfortable in the store, walking around and looking at clothing. I, on the other hand, was standing still, unsure of what to look at. I was afraid to pick something up that others might consider dorky or weird. I also had no clue what size I was anymore, as this was the first time I'd been shopping since I began treatment at the Renfrew Center and I knew that my weight had changed significantly.

Nevertheless I decided to try on pants. I found a random pair of jeans and decided to use them to determine my new pants size. Krista watched as I pulled several of the largest sizes off the rack and headed toward the dressing room.

"Where are you going with those?" she asked me.

"I'm trying to find my new pants size," I told her.

"Are you sure that's a good idea?"

"I have to know."

"Those are not going to fit," she said with a smile.

Astounded I asked her, "You think I need them even *bigger*?" I was near tears.

"No," she answered patiently, "*smaller.*"

I didn't believe her, but it felt good to hear. I let her put back the very largest sizes, since the only reason I took those was in order to make sure that at least something would be too big on me. I wanted to work my way down from the largest sizes to the smaller ones. I thought that way I would feel better about my new size. Krista did not approve of my reasoning. I kept the sizes that I thought might actually fit and took them, along with the new smaller sizes Krista gave me, to the dressing room where I tried them on. I was sure Krista was out of her mind for giving me pants so small. But every single pair was too *large*. I was happily surprised!

"I was prepared for this!" Krista called from the outside of my dressing room, "Here!" She tossed a couple pairs of even smaller pants over the door. I tried on the bigger pair first. It was still too large. Then I tried the smaller pair. Krista warned me that this pair was going to fit more tightly and to be ready for that. I mentally prepared myself and put on the pants. They fit. Tightly. The way jeans are *supposed* to fit. I came out of the dressing room. Krista had known all along that these were the right pair!

"Wow! How did you do that?" I asked, impressed.

"I know pants," Krista said.

Our next stop was the food court where everyone ordered a snack. Except for me. Suddenly I got it in my head that I could not order anything. I wouldn't eat or drink anything and I wouldn't buy any clothes. I was sinking into old thinking patterns and I felt trapped, but I couldn't seem to break free. Compared to Renfrew the mall was so loud and chaotic. It seemed to me at the time that my old thinking patterns and behaviors would somehow protect me, even though at the same time they were causing me great unhappiness. A girl named Suzanne came over and offered me a granola bar. I declined her offer and felt miserable.

We continued shopping and I continued walking around feeling overwhelmed. We entered a store called Express. It was noisy and crowded and the music was loud and booming. I began to cry. This was the first time I'd been outside of the treatment center walls in two months and I longed for the safety and security I felt back at Renfrew. I tried on the items necessary to complete the assignment and resigned myself to going home empty-handed.

Our last stop was Nordstrom. It was nearing the end of our trip and I still hadn't bought or eaten anything. Finally

I decided that I had to at least break free of my self-imposed food prison.

Before I could change my mind I went over to Suzanne. I told her how I'd decided back at the food court not to eat anything and not to buy anything. I told her how sad and deprived I now felt because of it.

"You haven't eaten anything?" she asked me, surprised.

"No."

"Here, I still have the granola bar!" Suzanne pulled out her granola bar and cheerfully offered it to me.

"Oh, I don't know..."

"*Take it!*"

I thanked Suzanne and took the granola bar. I ate it and felt a sudden rush of freedom. I was breaking an eating disorder "rule" and it felt liberating! Since I had missed my supervised fluids at Renfrew, I also got vitamin water. I was eating outside of Renfrew for the first time! I felt so proud of myself.

But my joy was short-lived. Upon my return to Renfrew I felt self-disgust at how easily I'd "caved" and given in to eating when it was not absolutely necessary. I had trouble at dinner that night. I panicked in the line and cried. I didn't know what to get. I never wanted to eat again. I felt as though I'd already eaten what I could "afford" to eat at the mall. How could I eat again so soon afterwards? I wanted a fruit but since it wasn't required according to my meal plan, I did not get one. Again I felt deprived. I asked for staff support and ate in the community room. I was so uncomfortable with the fact that I was doing well!

I was really feeling the loss of my eating disorder. It felt as though a part of me, albeit a very unhealthy part of me, was being lost forever. In a sense my anorexia had been my closest friend and only true relationship for so long that it was difficult and painful to let go. My eating disorder had provided me with a sense of power and self-control and I was afraid of who I would be without it. I also feared that my eating disorder was what made me special and unique, and that by giving it up I would lose all of the support I had gained when I was sick. I sat down and wrote in my journal:

> I forget the dangers and glorify anorexia... I'm afraid to get better because I'm afraid I will lose the intense support I have when I'm sick. Most people seem to need the most support when they are sad, but [right now] I need it most when I am happy... I'm afraid of happiness and of doing well or even okay. It's foreign and unfamiliar and I feel vulnerable and unstable, as if I was stepping out onto thin ice and could crash at any moment. I feel alone. When I'm doing poorly at Renfrew the staff pays attention to me... I'm jealous of others who get attention for being sick or sad or having a hard time. I worry that my medicine is responsible for my progress and newfound emotional stability...

I sat with my journal for a little while after I finished writing. I wanted very much to break down and have a contact. I eventually did speak to a staff member. Although I wanted even more staff support, I reminded myself that I was on level three for a reason. I could handle this.

I wrote a letter to Jackie about my experience at the mall. I also came up with some positive statements to put things into perspective:

"I am not a number."

"Sizes measure clothing, not me."

"I don't judge myself for my blood pressure – weight is just another number."

To further challenge my unhealthy thoughts about weight and body image, and to prove to me that my body image was distorted, Brenda signed me up for an individual art therapy session with Kim.

Kim and I completed a project called a "body tracing." I entered the room and saw a very large sheet of white paper taped to the wall. Kim gave me a pencil and instructed me to draw the outline of what I perceived to be my body image. When I was finished she asked me if I wanted to make any changes. Then I drew over the pencil markings with a permanent marker to be able to see the outline better.

When the outline of what I thought my body was shaped like was finished I stood against the picture and Kim traced my body in another colored permanent marker. We filled in the outline of the accurate shape and compared my distorted body image to what I actually looked like. It was quite eye opening. I had drawn myself significantly larger than I in fact was. I had been terrified that I would be larger than I thought I was and in reality I was *smaller*!

We then did a similar exercise with strings. I tied strings into circles I thought would fit around different parts of my body and then Kim took the actual measurements with new strings. Every single time my strings were longer than Kim's, indicating that my body was smaller than I had imagined. I realized that measuring my worth with a faulty measuring stick was silly. And I was worth more than my body shape and size anyway!

I felt very good as I left the art studio that day.

A few years ago a documentary called *Thin* was filmed at Renfrew. It followed the residential treatment of four Renfrew residents, showing the struggles and difficulties the women faced in their recoveries. Although it was a powerful film and had many good points, *Thin* contained details of specific weights and calories and was at times a very graphic and triggering movie.

As part of cinema-therapy two we would watch it and participate in group discussions involving thoughts and feelings that came up for us during the viewing. I had a very difficult time with this movie.

We were supposed to eat a snack while we watched. I had difficulty with that assignment. I barely ate anything at all. I cried a lot. In a way I wanted to keep crying in order to be noticed, in order not to feel lost somehow in the chaos of the movie and the emotion in the room. I tried to show the others in the room – through my tears, not my voice – that the movie was difficult for me to see. I also got into "competition mode," crying even during parts of the movie that did not bother me personally. If someone else cried, I cried. I had to, in a sense, "keep up." Some parts of the movie hit uncomfortably close to home. Other things in the movie triggered me only because I let them. I found it very difficult to see my therapist and my nutritionist, Brenda and Jackie, taking care of other patients, not even knowing that I exist.

For much of the movie I was not mentally present. I was thinking about my own eating disorder history, self-harm, and how my social life in Israel had been wrecked over my obsession with food. I wasn't even looking at the screen anymore. I was miserable. Finally Krista, the counselor running the group, asked me to step out of the room with her for a moment.

We talked in the upstairs hallway just outside the level four lounge where the movie was still going on. At first I was silent, although my thoughts were racing.

"Do you not want to process with me because you're afraid you'll look like you're not as far along in your recovery?" Krista asked me. "Because I know better."

She looked at me expectantly. I told her what I was thinking: I felt as though I had missed out by never having reached a lower weight. I felt inadequate, not "good enough" at my eating disorder. I figured that meant I would have to relapse again and next time I would aim for an even lower weight. I told Krista about my struggles with the snack. Memories of old habits were triggered by the movie and I wanted to engage in eating-disordered behaviors. Who was I without them? I went on and on, telling Krista my worries and fears.

In essence I was still struggling with my identity. It was hard to recover. Who was I without my eating disorder? When I had finished, Krista advised me to journal.

I took my journal and went downstairs to my usual journaling spot – the bench outside the team center. But on my way to the couch I saw Jackie talking to another girl and feelings of jealousy welled up in me once more. I kept remembering the painful thoughts and feelings I had experienced during the movie, which came raging back full force, and suddenly I was in a panic.

Jackie noticed that I was hurting. She asked me what was wrong. I told her that we had just watched *Thin*. She seemed surprised that I was this distraught over the movie. I was frustrated and angry with my inability to communicate effectively. Jackie asked again what was wrong. I told her I was angry. Jackie asked me again and again why I was angry but I couldn't think of a "good" answer. Instead I cried harder, feeling trapped. Finally, I felt as though I had to get out.

I became panicky and my heart was racing. I started to hyperventilate and walked briskly out the door and onto the patio, my head pounding. Jackie followed me asking, "What just happened?" and "What's wrong?" But I couldn't focus my thoughts and think of answers for her. I kept crying. I just really did not want her to go away.

Jackie calmly said that it's very difficult to talk to me when I'm worked up like this. She said it was clear what I should do and that the answer was in my hands. I looked down and realized I was still holding my journal. I knew immediately that she was correct.

"It's your outlet," Jackie told me. "Write."

I went back inside and began to journal. I quickly calmed down. Through my writing I realized that I had inadvertently reverted to using drama as a means to get attention. Understanding that people make mistakes, I resolved to learn from this experience and not let it happen again.

Later that evening I sat on the bench outside the team center with Krista. I was still emotionally in "competition mode" after seeing the documentary. Specifically, I was jealous of the low body weight of one of the girls in the movie. I knew Krista had known the girl when she was at Renfrew. I knew I probably shouldn't ask what was on my mind, but I felt I couldn't keep the question in any longer.

"How tall was she?" I asked Krista. Krista gave me a rough estimate. I thought for a moment, doing some brief calculations, and then smiled. I was significantly taller and therefore our weight percentiles had been comparable. My mood lifted. I felt that in some small way I deserved treatment if, after all, my weight compared to the girl in the movie.

"So I *was* as sick as her!" I blurted out.

Krista looked at me and said solemnly, "Congratulations." She said it in such a way that, although I *was* proud of my "accomplishment," I felt guilty. I told her so.

"I'm not apologizing for that," Krista said. "You are making this a private victory in your head and I am congratulating you." Krista communicated to me that no one can "make" me feel guilty – or any other feeling. My feelings are my responsibility, not to be blamed on others. She also said she wasn't sorry I felt guilty.

I thought about what she was saying. I knew it was good for me to feel bad about this because that meant I didn't want to define myself in terms of weight and sickness. I did not want to identify myself by my eating disorder.

Not anymore.

I thought about who I was. Not as an eating disorder patient, but as a person. I thought about what I wanted to accomplish. I resolved to work hard and strengthen my skills and come out of this on the other side, able to help myself and others. Although I was determined to overcome my emotional neediness and learn to self-soothe, I felt incapable of soothing *anyone*, let alone *myself.* I found myself comparing myself to others again. But this time it was not to others with eating disorders. Instead I was comparing myself to those who help women and girls with eating disorders recover.

I thought about Brenda. Could I do her job, I wondered? Often Brenda had let our therapy sessions run over the set amount of time. She never made me leave her office before I was ready and composed. One time Brenda had car trouble and didn't make it in to work until later in the afternoon. *That* day she had stayed at Renfrew hours and hours longer than usual, ensuring that she saw every patient on her schedule. It was not uncommon for her to schedule mini meetings with patients who needed a little extra support. *That* is the kind of commitment and care that Brenda has for the people with whom she works. I wanted to be like that. I wanted to truly care about and help people.

I thought about Brenda and Jackie and the others at Renfrew. They all have such positive attitudes and ways of communicating with people. I wanted to be like that. I looked to Brenda and Jackie as positive role models in my life. In high spirits I wrote in my journal:

I'm going to try to absorb all of the positive things and learn from Brenda and Jackie – to come away from Renfrew healthier and more balanced. I know it won't be easy at times, but people here seem to have a lot of faith in me. Maybe I can learn to have faith in myself... I know that in time, if I stay really determined, I can do it.

Fully resolute in my efforts to become more positive and self-supporting, I informed staff of my desire to take care of myself. I told them that if I came for a contact they should first encourage me to try to manage by myself. They all agreed.

In addition to easing up on my reliance on staff support, I reached out to my fellow residents, including Faith, my five-minute roommate from my first day at Renfrew. We had recently begun spending more time together during the morning exercise group. We'd walk around the paved path around the parking lot together and talk. Faith was a very bright, talented and fascinating person. She studied languages and religions. She had a wealth of knowledge inside of her. She was also very physically strong. She could do a type of lunge I'd never even seen before and when I tried it I ended up on the floor. She often complained that she couldn't be diagnosed anorexic because her muscles brought her over the weight range for anorexia, even though she was still dangerously underweight and had far too little body fat.

Apart from her eating disorder, Faith had a troubled past. She couldn't remember very much of her traumatic childhood but was slowly unraveling horrific mysteries in therapy. She called upon friends and her religious faith to help her through difficult times.

Through our time spent together, Faith and I became friends.

On Sunday July 15, I took my first pass with Faith. A pass is an allotted amount of time during which a Renfrew resident is allowed to leave the Renfrew grounds to an agreed upon location. Faith and I filled out our pass forms indicating where we were going, what therapeutic goals we had, and how we were going to reach those goals. We were planning to go to Target, a store that sold everything from clothing to kitchenware. My therapeutic goal was to purchase something for myself, something I seldom did, as I never seemed to feel "worth it." In addition, I was taking a roll of film from Israel to be developed. I was very excited to see my pictures from Israel, although I was mildly concerned about how I might look in those pictures. I had been very sick when they were taken. I had extremely mixed feelings about the pictures, as I wrote in my journal:

> I'm going to Target... I'm taking my Israel pictures to be developed. I hope they're not horribly triggering, but in a way I *want* them to be. I was really sick then and I want props for it. Maybe that sounds sick or bad or something, but that's how I feel and this is *my* journal so I'll write what I want. That's the truth.

Many things went wrong on our supposed three-hour pass. Right from the start it did not go as expected. We were supposed to meet another girl at Renfrew who would be driving us. But she didn't show. After hanging around in the Renfrew lobby waiting, and watching as our pass time dwindled, we finally decided after an hour to just go without her. We got a ride to Target with Danielle and a few other girls who were also on pass. We planned to take a cab home.

The second thing that went wrong was that we did not actually *stay*, like we were supposed to, at Target. Instead, upon learning that this Target did not do one-hour photo processing, we walked down the road and across the street to a drugstore. It was at this point that I realized I had accidentally walked out of Target carrying merchandise I had not purchased. Hurriedly, I went back to Target, returned the product, and we continued on our way to the drugstore. We walked quickly down the street, dodged traffic, climbed over the street railing, pushed our way through some bushes, and finally arrived at Walgreen's.

I walked up to the counter with my roll of film and asked when my pictures would be ready. The man said that I could pick them up at around 6:00 pm. We had to be back at Renfrew by 6:00 pm, so I practiced my assertiveness skills.

"You advertise one-hour photo processing," I told the man. "It is now 4:45 pm. I need those pictures at 5:45 pm." Much to my surprise, he agreed. I came back at 5:45 pm and picked them up. I stared at the pictures, longing to look more like I had in Israel. Although I wanted to have a healthy identity, it was still difficult not to mentally compare my current self with the girl in the pictures. I flipped through them repeatedly, obsessing over my thin, ill body. Faith called for a cab, and I continued to stare at the photographs while we waited.

That's when more trouble began. We called a cab and waited for it outside of Walgreen's. We waited and waited. It did not seem to be coming. At first we had been waiting for the cab outside, but soon a thundering crash of lightning sent us back inside. I felt good that my first instinct was to pull Faith inside to safety.

6:00 pm rolled by with no sign of the cab. We called again. We called Renfrew to let them know we were okay. It wasn't until about 8:15 pm that our cab finally arrived. It turned out that the company had sent it to Wal-Mart instead of Walgreen's.

We got back to Renfrew and had a very late dinner, and then I continued to obsess over my pictures. I wanted to get a contact to discuss my being triggered by them, but after talking it over with Danielle I decided to work on being more self-supporting. I was making progress. Danielle told me that she'd gone through a similar experience with her own old photos and that Brenda had really helped her. She advised me to take my pictures with me to my next therapy session.

I met with Brenda the next day. Following Danielle's advice I brought along my pictures and showed them to her, asking her what she thought of them. Brenda and I went through the pictures, one by one, and she pointed out the deadness in my eyes.

She looked at one picture and said, "You're in so much pain here, can't you see it?" She looked at another and said, "You look like a crack addict!" I shot her a look. "No, seriously," she maintained. "Look at your eyes. Your mouth is smiling but your eyes are nervous and jittery. Your body is emaciated. This is *sick*, Naomi." I looked at the picture. I still thought I looked better then than now.

Brenda told me that holding on to these pictures was equivalent to holding on to my eating disorder. She asked me to give them to her. She would keep them in a sealed envelope in her office until I was ready to go home. I was not thrilled with the idea but I nevertheless gave her the pictures. And afterwards, although I was upset, rather than going for a contact, I self-soothed and talked to my friends.

Although I was doing well in overcoming my emotional neediness and insecurity, I still had a few off days. However, each time I slipped it was less intense and I subsequently learned and gained valuable life experience as I went along.

After meeting with Brenda and having my pictures confiscated, I was feeling pretty down. It seemed I *needed* those pictures. They were *mine*! I did not like that Brenda took them from me. Furthermore, I did not like that she'd said I was holding on to my eating disorder by keeping them, especially since I suspected she was right.

I cried through my next group. I took a nap, falling asleep and staying asleep through two groups. When I woke up I was still very upset. A staff member offered to have a contact with me. I declined, explaining that I was working on self-soothing, although I was very bitter about it. Eventually I was so overwhelmed by trying to manage my feelings of loneliness and anger alone that I knew I needed to talk to someone. I went to Jackie's office.

I knocked on Jackie's door.

"Come in!" she called.

I entered her office and didn't know what to say. I wanted to express how frustrated I felt and how overwhelming the process of recovery had become. I wanted to convey, through eye contact alone, that change is scary and that I was afraid. But of course glaring at Jackie got me nowhere.

"What's going on?" she asked.

I stood by her door crying. I told her I wanted to give up and quit treatment. We both knew better. I didn't really mean what I was saying. I was overwhelmed and didn't know what else to say. I wanted company. I felt so alone.

Jackie looked at me and said, "You are very overwhelmed." She said in an empathetic and kind way, "I'm not listening to your words."

I paused and then said, "Please help me!"

"What would you like me to do?" she asked. I thought for a moment. I didn't know what she *could* do to help. But I felt cared about when I was in her office. I felt less alone. It was soothing.

"How much longer are you staying?" I asked Jackie. It was already after 5:00 pm.

"About ten more minutes," she told me.

"Can I stay with you?" I asked her.

"Yes."

I stayed with Jackie while she finished up her work for the day. She took a phone call from the kitchen, finished writing her notes, and then told me she had to make photocopies in the team center. She asked if I wanted to walk with her. Of course I said yes.

On the way from her office to the team center Jackie told me it was normal to feel the way I did and to have trouble self-soothing – it's just that most people deal with these emotional issues when they are younger. Jackie told me that when she was a little girl she used to go to sleep-away camp in the summer. She said that during the first few nights, every year, she would sit up and cry for her mom and dad, but that eventually she was okay. She said that everyone goes through this – feeling lonely and vulnerable when they are by themselves. It's normal. She told me I would be okay. She also told me that it's okay to have *some* contacts. It's about balance. Jackie asked me to think about what balance means to me.

When we finished talking I felt better and more self-confident. I knew I would be okay. I smiled at Jackie. "Thank you for caring," I told her.

She smiled back.

8

Week Eight: Triumph Over Triggers

Sometimes you will see or hear things that may cause you to want to engage in eating-disordered behaviors. It may be anything from seeing a magazine ad to hearing comments made by others. You will not be able to prevent all triggers. You can, however, choose how you respond.

How to

Recognize triggers for what they are. A trigger is anything that sparks an urge to engage in unhealthy behaviors. Challenge your thoughts. Find healthy ways to think about the trigger. Explore your deeper feelings. A trigger is not catastrophic and does not mean certain failure or symptoms. You still have choices.

When to use this skill

When you feel triggered.

*P*art of the level three program is a trip to the grocery store every other week. The goal of the shopping trip is to teach patients how to shop for groceries in a more normalized way, not choosing foods based on calorie or fat content alone. Instead a Renfrew nutritionist leads the group, teaching about various nutrients and "legitimate" reasons to choose one food over another – such as taste preference, price, and nutritional value. On Wednesday July 18, I was to take my first group tour of the grocery store. I was in a bad mood that day and did not want to go. I wrote in my journal before we left:

> I don't want to go to the supermarket. I don't want to obsess over food labels and never want to eat again. I already am not in an eating kind of mood... I'm nervous about the supermarket trip...

Then, just as we were about to leave, the girl who was supposed to mentor two new patients that night asked me if I would do it instead of her since she wanted to go out. I enjoyed mentoring new patients so I assured her it was no problem. I had already met one of the new patients and I liked her. Then I met the second new patient and my whole attitude changed.

The woman was literally skeletal. I had never seen anyone so thin in my entire life. I only had enough time to introduce myself before it was time to leave for the store. On the way to the supermarket other girls were talking about how triggered they felt by the new patient. I felt triggered too. I also felt angry. I did not like seeing anyone who was "better" at her eating disorder than I was, as judged by thinness and low body weight. I felt inadequate. Anorexia had been mine.

At once I knew Brenda was right in taking my pictures away from me. But I didn't care. I still felt beaten. I was never "sick enough." If anorexia was a contest, the new patient had clearly won. For the first time in a very long while, I was comparing myself and my condition to another patient. It did not feel good. I was very distressed at the thought of mentoring the new patient that night. I felt conflicted. On the one hand I wanted to avoid the new patient completely out of jealousy and anger. But on the other hand I knew that she had done nothing to me and that she had come to Renfrew to recover. It was a confusing mess of feelings.

I struggled throughout the supermarket tour and when we got back I went straight to Jackie's office. I walked into her office and sat down in the chair next to her desk. Very upset, I told her that I was triggered by the new patient and asked for support. How was I supposed to mentor this girl when I felt so triggered by her?

"Naomi," Jackie said, "you are triggered by everything! Everything triggers you! You see a tree and you're triggered!"

I glared at her.

"I'm serious," Jackie persisted. "You need to understand that you are not made of glass. People should not have to walk on eggshells around you. You won't break if you are triggered. You are strong, Naomi. You don't need to be triggered."

I cried, not believing her. Frustrated and unable to think of anything productive to say on the subject I demanded to know my weight.

"I'm not telling you," she said.

"Tell me my weight Jackie!" I shouted. "Tell me my weight! That is *my* number and I need to know now!" I cried and I shouted and I begged, but Jackie wouldn't budge.

"You can cry and scream and stand on your head if you want to," Jackie explained, "But I'm not telling you. You know when I say no it's no." Jackie threatened to send me out into the hall if I didn't calm down and speak rationally.

Unable to talk numbers with Jackie, I resorted to the only thing left – talking about what was really going on.

"I'm so frustrated, Jackie!" I cried, "I feel like I can't do anything without someone holding my hand!"

"Am I holding your hand?" she asked, her eyes widening in surprise.

"*Yes!*"

"I'm not holding your hand – I'm kicking your butt!" said Jackie. "I won't tell you your weight and I threatened to kick you out of my office – this is not hand holding!"

Taking a deep breath, I told Jackie my concerns about mentoring the new patient.

"Listen, Naomi," said Jackie, "She is just a sick girl who came here to get well. You are in a position to help her. You have the opportunity to make her feel welcome and give her a positive first experience." Jackie talked to me about strength and choice and how she believes in me.

Put that way, I felt empowered. From now on I wouldn't think of the new patient as a trigger, but rather as someone I was in the position to help. I really liked Jackie. Talking to her always seemed to put me in a better place mentally and emotionally. I had a lot of respect for her and I decided to confide in her something that had been a major source of motivation in my recovery.

"Jackie," I said, "I want you to know that sometimes it can get really hard and I feel down on myself and I don't feel like I deserve recovery. But during those times I remember all the hard work you've done on my behalf – all of the time and effort *you* have put into my recovery – and I think to myself that even if I can't do this for myself, I will at least give you a success story."

Jackie smiled. "I appreciate it," she said. "I really appreciate it. You're a good kid."

That night I mentored the two new patients. The girl I was concerned about mentoring *did* say some potentially triggering things. But I remembered Jackie telling me that I am strong and don't need to be triggered. I remembered that I was not made of glass and would not break if something triggering was said. I answered the new girl's questions as best I could.

"What if I get fat?" she asked me.

"They won't let that happen here," I assured her.

"How do *you* trust that?" she retorted.

"Because they *haven't* let it happen," I told her.

After I finished mentoring I sat and talked to another girl who was having a hard night until she felt better. Twice in a row I set aside my fear of triggers in the interest of helping others. I learned to think about triggers in a new light and actually use them to my advantage, exploring what lay beneath my feeling triggered. And I emerged stronger for it and able to help others. I felt so good being able to help others and thought that this must be the feeling the staff get when they are able to help. In that moment I knew that I had to recover and use my experience to help girls who are struggling the way I had.

9

Week Nine: Have Integrity

Integrity requires a full and fearless commitment to living according to your beliefs. It means accepting who you are and not expecting everyone to like you or approve of you all the time. It means doing what's right even when what's right isn't popular. This is one of the most important skills in your recovery, for it is the antithesis of living in accordance with the dictates of an eating disorder. Through integrity, relationships can be rebuilt and your life can be made whole.

How to

Be honest and don't mislead. Take personal responsibility. Everyone makes mistakes – take responsibility for correcting yours. Don't play games or manipulate. If you have made a mistake have the courage to admit it, correct it, and learn from it. Be accountable for your own actions. Be stronger than peer pressure and stress. Have the courage to be your true self.

When to use this skill

Always.

*a*t Renfrew there are specialized groups on Thursdays which address the struggles of each specific eating disorder. Since I struggled with anorexia I attended a group called "Anorexic Eating Patterns."

"Welcome to 'Anorexic Eating Patterns,'" began the group facilitator, Rachel. "This is a group for those of you who tend to use restriction as a primary form of coping." I looked around the room. All eyes were glued to Rachel. She was an awesome counselor and people looked forward to her group all week.

"Today," she continued, "we are going to discuss integrity." She looked around the room. "Now, how many of you think you have integrity? Raise your hands." A fair number of hands went up.

"Okay, put your hands down," said Rachel. "Get ready for this – *none* of you have integrity." Looks of discouragement and hurt appeared on the faces of many who had raised their hands, mine included.

"Who can tell me why you don't have integrity?" Rachel asked the group. Danielle raised her hand. "Yes, Danielle?"

Danielle answered, "Because we have eating disorders and you can't have an eating disorder *and* integrity at the same time."

"Very good, Danielle," said Rachel. "Now, some of you are wondering why, aren't you?" Rachel went on to explain that when someone has an eating disorder she is, by definition, being dishonest in at least some way – lying about food intake or not sharing the fact that she has an eating disorder, for example. She continued talking about integrity and that in order to truly regain our integrity we must first fully recover from our eating disorders, which, as she often told us, "is a choice."

Rachel's integrity talk drove me crazy and I pondered it for a very long time. It became the theme of my day. I went to MST that afternoon still pondering integrity. Then I did something for which I felt extremely hypocritical.

For the preceding three or so meals, I hadn't finished all of my salad dressing. At first it was innocent enough. I just left a thin layer in the little plastic cup. It was more normal, I reasoned, to leave a little bit behind than to scrape up every last drop. But at the next meal I found myself leaving more dressing behind. And so it continued. Now at MST, I finished almost none of my dressing. Instead I hid it and continued my meal. I didn't think much of not finishing my dressing. It was well hidden, but I was sitting right next to Brenda. After the meal she motioned toward my partially full container of salad dressing and asked me to finish it.

"It'll be easy," she coached, "just a little bit more."

"I'd rather not," I said.

"Come on, I could finish that in one bite!"

"No. Because it's not just that..." Awkwardly I took the rest of the dressing out of its hiding place and showed it to her.

The table looked at me in silence. No one dared to say a word. Finally Brenda spoke.

"Naomi," she said seriously, "it is one thing not to finish your meal, but it's another thing to hide it..."

"I didn't hide it!" I said, "I just *showed* it to you!" I convinced myself that it was not a lie and that I hadn't truly hidden it. After all, if I wanted to hide it I would not show her the rest of my dressing!

"...and it's quite another thing to *lie* about hiding it."
Brenda looked at me. The table of girls looked at me. I felt
really low. Brenda inspected my trash to make sure I hadn't
hidden any other food. No one had done that to me since I
was required to have my tray inspected routinely by staff. I
had recently moved up in the meal levels and was trusted to
make healthy decisions at mealtimes. Now I felt mistrusted
and low. I thought about Rachel and integrity. I thought
back to her session during which she accused us of not
having integrity. I was now glad that she drove me crazy
with it, because it forced me to look deeper, to discover that
what I needed was not integrity on a basic, simple level, but
rather integrity of a different kind – a full, fearless kind of
integrity. I still had to come to terms with the fact that not
everyone is going to like me or approve of me all of the time.
Regardless of the consequences I had to act with integrity.
I had truly believed I had integrity, at least at the level of
telling the truth. But now it seemed I had to rethink that
belief.

No! I would not let myself off that easy! I *did* have integrity and I would regain it. I decided to take responsibility and
fix this. I had learned that I can always fix things from the
time I threatened to run away. I would take what I learned
that night and apply it to this situation, as I had applied it
to many situations before.

After lunch I went to after-meal process. Since I was on
level three, it was an optional group. But I felt that it would
be the right thing to do under the circumstances – to explore, in a group setting, what had happened and to learn
from it.

I came out of after-meal process a little more secure.
After I shared the story of my slip-up and my fears about
losing my integrity with the group, I received support from
the other girls in after-meal process. They told me they were
proud of me for taking responsibility. One girl who had been

in my MST group told me that I didn't *have* to show Brenda the rest of my salad dressing, and that that in itself demonstrated integrity. No one felt that I was a bad example to the community, which I had feared they would. No one was disappointed in me or thought less of me. Girls opened up about their own struggles. I felt far less alone and more confident in my ability to set things right.

After the process group I headed over to Brenda's office and knocked on her door. Brenda opened the door and invited me inside for a few minutes.

"This is hard..." I stammered, "I lied to you..."

"About hiding the dressing?" she asked, not surprised.

"Yes."

"I know."

We spoke briefly about the incident and how I had learned to be really careful with my eating habits. Maybe for some people it was okay, even normal, to leave behind some salad dressing. But for me, in my situation, it was not. Because as I learned, one slip can lead to another and another – each more serious than the last. It was good that I caught myself early on.

I told Brenda that I wanted to own up to what I had done and take responsibility, to regain my integrity. I told her I was taking corrective measures. Specifically, I had gone to after-meal process, I had confessed to Brenda, and I was planning to ask for community support.

Then we spoke about my chances at getting level four the following week.

"Don't count on it," she said.

Giving me level four that week might send the wrong message to others who had been completely honest in their recoveries and who had not lied or hidden food. In addition, my actions and behavior, not just today, showed that I was not yet ready for level four.

That night, just as many nights before, I struggled with feelings of loneliness and emotional neediness. I reminded myself that I wanted this. I wanted to be able to take care of myself. When I first came to Renfrew I could barely even survive on my own – Nina once had to help me regulate my breathing! I had learned to self-soothe more and more as time went on. First that meant asking for a contact when I had difficult feelings. Then it meant getting to the root of the issues and not asking for needless contacts. Now it meant trying to soothe myself *without* a contact. I felt lonely and sad and longed for a contact, but instead I took out my journal and I wrote. Normally I wrote in my journal on the bench outside the team center, but now I wrote in my room:

> I'm journaling in my room because it is too painful to be outside the team center, knowing I shouldn't go for a contact. This is so incredibly painful. Especially knowing that it probably won't even get me to level four. But I have to do it for me. It's hard but if it works it will be worth it. It's an investment in the rest of my life. This is painful but it's growth… Tonight is so hard. It's taking everything I've got. I look in the mirror and see a fat girl. I'm so scared. That wasn't there before! I want to go to sleep just because I don't want to be awake anymore!

Despite my pain, I had a breakthrough that night. Instead of isolating, going to sleep, and "escaping" I went out into the hallway and found a group of girls. I sat with Melanie, Danielle, and Faith and shared my struggles with them. I told them how difficult it was for me not to go to staff for support. Then we talked and laughed and hung out and I really felt better. My first instinct was to run downstairs and tell staff what I had accomplished. But I stopped myself. Keeping it to myself, at least for now, was part of becoming my own "home base."

I went into the following day on a high note. I felt confident in my newfound ability to deal with my feelings without staff assistance. I looked forward to telling Brenda about my success, hoping in some way that it would convince her that I really *was* ready for level four after all.

I got some hard news that day which put all of my coping skills into immediate use: my insurance company no longer felt I needed treatment at the residential level. Usually Brenda conducted my insurance reviews but since she was coming in later that day Joy, the red team leader, conducted my review this time.

Insurance is a tricky little game when it comes to residential eating disorder treatment. Policies vary widely between companies – and even *within* companies. Some give wonderful coverage and benefits. Others do not. Often girls are forced to leave treatment early because insurance cuts out on them. When that happens – and it happens with great frequency – it is tragic. It deprives people of the help they have so desperately needed and finally found. Some don't even get the chance to enter treatment at all. It can literally destroy lives.

My insurance company was wonderful throughout my entire treatment process, covering the vast majority of treatment costs and thus allowing me to receive much needed help. The truth was that at this point, although there were certainly still struggles and challenges to overcome, I *was* doing well. And all hope of staying was not lost. I would be starting the Days Transitional Living Arrangement program and staying for an additional two weeks, paying only for room and board. It was a really good deal. Hearing this, however, caused great turmoil in my mind. My first reaction to the news that I would soon be going home was great distress and the urge to self-sabotage. If I regressed, I reasoned incorrectly, they'd have to let me stay! In fact, looking back I now see my slip up in MST as an instance of acting out on this theory, although I didn't know for sure at the time that insurance would not renew my residential stay. Instead of acting out on my self-sabotaging thoughts, I sat down and immediately wrote in my journal. I did not want to lose my integrity through actions I would certainly regret later. Instead I would act in healthy ways, using my skills. I tried to capture my feelings and write about them rather than act them out the way I had done several weeks before. I wrote:

> I have so many feelings in me. I'm angry, I'm indignant, I'm ashamed, and I feel like a spoiled brat. I want to make a huge scene and completely sabotage my recovery and never eat again. I want to break all the rules and get back on full day room. I want to cut and scream and sleep for a long, long time. I heard them talking about me in the team center saying that Days is "effective immediately..." No warning! Just like that! They're still talking about me! I'm so mad and angry and sad and hurt. I feel betrayed. I trusted them to keep me here. Maybe Brenda would have gotten me to stay, if she was here...

Then I reflected on the situation and wrote, more rationally:

> I know they did the best they could. Instead of causing a huge disaster to get attention and all that, I am trying so hard to use my skills. My insides are on fire and I want to explode but I'm using my skills. I talked to Melanie, I did art, and I'm writing....

Another way in which I dealt with my feelings was to buy a Renfrew sweatshirt. It was a way to symbolically "wrap myself up" in Renfrew. I wrote in my journal: "This is called clinging to Renfrew for dear life!"

Although I was doing well in my recovery, I still had very little faith in myself. Instead, I considered myself unready to return home. I felt I still needed Renfrew for my very survival. After talking to Brenda over the following several days I made peace with the fact that I really was ready to go home soon. Brenda and I had a conference call with my parents and decided that August 3, Friday two weeks from now, would be a good discharge date. We all felt that it was important to have a definite plan for my return home.

Brenda assured me that she fully agreed with my discharge date, and that even if insurance had covered further treatment she wouldn't have kept me at Renfrew. She said that staying any longer would foster dependency. Brenda encouraged me, insisting that I was ready to continue my journey of recovery at home. It was time.

My next family session was intense. We discussed the fact that Brenda took away my photographs of myself from when I was very sick. She said again that "holding on to these pictures was holding on to my eating disorder." She had taken the pictures away from me in order to stop me from "romanticizing my eating disorder."

Another thing I learned during my family session that morning was the real reason my mother cried when she saw me for the first time upon my return home from Israel. I assumed it was because she was so happy to see me. The real reason was because she was horrified by how sick I looked. My mother cried again during our family session just remembering it. It was eye-opening.

I thought back to the pictures Brenda had confiscated and realized that the reason she took them was not because I looked sick in them, but rather because I still believed I looked better in those pictures than I did at that moment. Because of that belief the pictures were dangerous for me to have.

But the most important part of the session was the rec-
ognition and understanding of what I had been doing with
my eating disorder. During the course of discussion of various elements of my life and what lay in store for me in
the future, I expressed fears and concerns common to any
twenty-year-old. I was afraid of the unknown, of growing
up, of becoming an adult. I feared independence. I would be
making more and more life-changing decisions as the years
went by, and I was afraid to make a wrong choice.

"These are all just normal parts of growing up," my father
said matter-of-factly.

Crying, I replied, "I don't want to grow up! I'm not ready!"
I had very little faith in myself.

"Well," he challenged, "what's the alternative?"

"*Have an eating disorder and die!*" I cried. My eyes grew
wide. "That's what I was doing," I whispered in amaze-
ment and utter shock. "*That's what I was doing!*" I practically shouted, again and again. Brenda looked at me and
nodded.

I was afraid of life. I was afraid of confrontation with
others and of not getting what I needed, so it was easier not
to ask. It was difficult to cope in healthy ways and far easier
to resort to attention-seeking behaviors and forcing others
to take care of me. Life is full of challenges. It was easier to
sink into non-existence, comforted by the familiarity of the
eating disorder I had known for years.

It was a heartbreaking realization for me. But now it was
time to take charge. I would keep learning and growing. I
would fight the eating disorder with all my strength. I would
strengthen my integrity and learn to self-soothe once and
for all! The session strengthened my resolve to fight this
battle and win. And with my new determination, I knew I
could win the battle wherever I happened to find myself, be
it at Renfrew or at home.

1 0

Week Ten:
Embrace Change

From the day you are born you are changing. You learn to speak, learn to walk, and your interests change as you mature. You are never done growing. Life is a constant growth experience. And just as you are changing, so is the world around you. New opportunities arise that require leaps of faith and openness to new experiences. It is up to you to recognize these opportunities and take the chance.

How to

Allow yourself the gift of change. Recognize opportunity. Take risks and try new things. Live on life's terms and grow – change is beautiful.

When to use this skill

When opportunities arise.

I did very well on the less structured Days Transitional Living Arrangement program, which was essentially the same as the residential program other than it involved a few less groups and the schedules were on pink paper. The next time I struggled with difficult thoughts and feelings, a few days later, I succeeded in calming myself and dealing with it even without help from my friends. I remembered Brenda's instructions on counter journaling (see Chapter 4) and I took out my journal and wrote:

I keep worrying that to really recover I will need to relapse again and come back to Renfrew. Evidence that supports this is that both guest speakers here who were patients are doing well and have been here twice. Danielle [is doing well and] has been here twice. Another girl I know came to Renfrew twice – once in Philadelphia and once in Florida. She's doing great. A girl from the Renfrew documentary is doing well and has gone here twice. The second time you don't have to spend time getting familiar with certain things – you know what to expect. Everyone I know who is doing well did it twice!

Now I will counter journal: There is evidence that with each relapse recovery is less likely. Many people come back to Renfrew twice because they weren't ready the first time or because they left too early. I came because I wanted help. I wanted to get well and recover fully. I'm staying a long time and am leaving at an appropriate time when my team feels I am ready. I'm scared to leave and I have thoughts of sabotaging my recovery just so that I can come back to Renfrew. I'm jealous of the people who get to come back here. But I have to remember that I felt the same way about leaving the hospital [and I never want to go back there]. I took well to Renfrew (well, after the first week or so!) and I can take well to "real life" back home too. It's okay to be scared and it's okay to have self-sabotaging thoughts as long as I remember that they are just thoughts – and very misguided ones at that. It's okay as long as I do not act on the thoughts or dwell on them. I never want to be sick again. I never want to relapse. I have to stop romanticizing anorexia. And I have to keep in mind that Renfrew saved my life, but now it is time to *live* it.

When I finished writing I felt much better and far more confident in my recovering abilities. A couple of girls even asked me what I was doing and I explained counter journaling to them. They each responded by thanking me and saying that it would be a great tool for them to use in their own recoveries. I felt so good being able to help not only myself, but others as well. Continuing to think outside of myself, I decorated Brenda's door for her birthday. I made a giant sign that read "Happy Birthday!" I also cut up pieces of colored paper and taped them to her door as confetti. After her birthday had ended, Brenda moved the sign inside of her office, but told me she planned to keep the confetti on her door forever.

Since I was going home relatively soon, Jackie had me prepare a seven-day food plan for when I returned home, along with a grocery list and a detailed description of what dinner would be on my first night home. In the course of preparing my lists I discovered that it was neither as easy as I'd hoped, nor as difficult as I'd feared.

At my following nutrition meeting I presented my work to Jackie who critiqued and revised it. I thanked her for helping me, as I felt far better once the lists were finalized, and I apologized for my outburst the previous week, which we both knew even at the time I would come to regret. Jackie, as always, was very understanding. I also expressed my fears of returning home and being triggered by weight-related jokes and comments. Jackie reiterated that I am not fragile and will not break if something triggering is said. She said to be careful not to take such things to heart, as not all comments contain healthy messages. I remembered a weight-loss contest I'd had with my mother at one point during my teenage years. Jackie had been pretty appalled when I had told her about that one. She reminded me that not all messages we receive from our parents are healthy. She told me that contrary to my fears, I *am* strong enough to handle the "real world."

We also discussed my MST incident. Jackie had found out about it during team rounds that week.

"Why didn't you tell me about it?" she asked me.

"I forgot to bring it up," I assured her that I was not hiding it. It honestly had slipped my mind.

"Naomi," Jackie said, "I want you to know that backsliding now will not keep you at Renfrew longer." I thought about what she was saying. It was true. In part I *had* acted out due to my fear of leaving Renfrew. Jackie continued, "You have received a lot of nurturing here, but you can do this on your own. You're stronger than you think," she said. "Your biggest obstacle is your lack of self-confidence."

That same day I found a few more pictures of myself from when I was very sick. They were pictures of me, looking quite emaciated, in two different prom dresses at the mall before I had entered treatment at Renfrew. Instead of staring longingly at them and driving myself crazy, I recognized immediately what I needed to do. Taking the pictures to Brenda, I cried as I handed them over.

"I'm never going to look like that again!" I sobbed. Then thinking it over I added, "I *hope* I never look like that again!" But although I knew I was healthier now and looked objectively better, I still cried. Taking the pictures from me, Brenda gave me a compassionate look.

"You are grieving the loss of your eating disorder," she said kindly. "It's okay to cry and be sad."

I thought about it and realized what a positive moment this was. I *was* grieving the loss of my eating disorder. And it *was* a significant loss. But *grieving* implied that I was truly giving it up this time. I felt reassured by that. Thinking of Jackie and her message that you only get one life, I told Brenda that I wanted to do great things with my life. She asked me to clarify my aspirations by writing them down, keeping in mind that they may change.

I thought about a group Rachel had once led. During the group she handed out tissues to each girl in the room.

"The tissue is your eating disorder," she had said. "I'm going to count to three and when I reach three I want you to do something with it." On the count of three some girls tore up their tissues. Others stuffed their tissues in their pockets. One girl blew her nose in her tissue. I folded mine into a pretty flower. My reason for doing so was simple: I wanted to learn and grow from my experience with my eating disorder. I wanted to transform it from something negative and life threatening into something positive and life affirming. My ambitions would reflect this desire.

After some consideration I wrote down the following goal: I want to work at a place like Renfrew; to help others the way I have been helped and to be the kind of person I admire.

It seemed to be an attainable goal and it was a goal that I wanted very much to achieve. I reviewed it with Brenda who agreed.

Thursday July 26 was a very good day for me. I woke up at 5:50 am for exercise B but accidentally turned off my alarm rather than hit snooze. So I got up at 7:00 am and was surprisingly okay with having missed exercise. Next, despite my not having exercised, I looked in the mirror and saw a thin, pretty girl smiling back at me. I was having a good body-image day! Since it was Thursday I got clean towels, which is always a perk. Amelia passed me the wand in inspiration celebration, meaning that the following week I would be running the show!

I got to go to the grocery store with a Renfrew nutritionist and another patient to help pick out food for that week's cooking group. I felt so normal at the store, shopping just like any other normal person, and not hyper focusing on the calories or fat content. I felt good. I could finally see the light at the end of this long, dark tunnel.

When I got back to Renfrew from the grocery store I sat down and decided to tackle my greatest fears regarding going home. I did it by making a chart:

Things I may struggle with	How I can cope	How my family can help
Meals, eating, food	Use distraction, separate emotions, remember my goals, remember Jackie.	Talk about things not food related. Stay calm, don't panic, don't make a big deal. Pep talk when needed, remind me that I can do this.
Exercise	Respect my body's limits.	Don't push exercise. Let me do what I think I need.

Chaos in the house	Take a "time out," do breathing exercises, be assertive about my boundaries.	Let me take a time out. Be supportive. Be as calm as possible.
Missing Renfrew	Journal, email, phone.	Listen, let me vent.
Feeling overwhelmed, anxious, alone, etc.	Journal, art, email, contact support people. Play with my rabbit or dog.	Spend time with me or give me space. But it is my job to communicate what it is that I need at that moment.

I planned to review the chart with my parents at my following family session.

Before leaving Renfrew I invited Jackie to one of my final family sessions. She said that she wasn't sure if she could make it, but that she would certainly try. After a lot of scheduling conflicts and changes, I was elated to walk into Brenda's office and see Jackie sitting in the chair across from the couch. She had made it! I felt so cared about! Jackie sat where Brenda usually sat when we did individual therapy, Brenda sat at the desk, and I sat on a wooden chair between them. We called my parents.

We discussed my fears of going home. We reviewed the chart I had made the day before. We discussed various options for my immediate future, such as starting school and getting a job. Jackie stressed the importance of seeing a nutritionist once a week. Everyone agreed that following my food plan is *my* responsibility and that no one can force me to eat. As for my fear of missing Renfrew, Jackie had a wonderful idea.

"I want to give you a transitional object," she said.

"What's that?" I asked.

"Something that was mine that you can hold on to that will remind you of me. It will help you feel connected even when you leave us."

"I want to give you one also," Brenda added.

I thought back to when my first therapist had moved away. She had knitted me a scarf before she left. Now I realized that had also been a transitional object. I looked at Brenda and Jackie and my eyes welled up with tears. To me, Jackie and Brenda represented recovery. Now I would have something concrete to hold on to and remember them by. It was all so thoughtful and kind. I felt truly cared about.

The following week Brenda gave me a Beanie Baby owl and Jackie gave me a small stuffed bear.

"I don't do this for many patients," Jackie told me, giving me a hug.

I told Jackie I would miss her. I asked her to sign my journal. She wrote me a touching message reminding me that I can take care of myself and recover. I was preparing to leave Renfrew and continue onward into my future. I knew I couldn't waste my time and energy on an eating disorder any longer.

Before I left, Jackie looked up and reminded me, "One life."

The following day I walked into team rounds confident that I had finally earned level four. As I took my seat at the front of the room, I noticed that everyone was smiling. I looked at Brenda.

"Naomi," she began, "there are no words to describe how proud of you I am. You've done great work here and you've exceeded my greatest expectations. Congratulations, you have earned level four."

The entire room of therapists, nutritionists, doctors, and nurses applauded. It was a fabulous moment. Later I volunteered to share the story of my recovery with the other Renfrew residents in a group later that week in order to provide inspiration and hope.

Two days before my discharge date, Sophia, my relatively new upstairs roommate, Brianne, and I went out on pass to the movies. We were given special permission to be out until 10:00 pm. We were to see a specific movie that we'd written down on our pass forms and gotten approved by our treatment teams. However, when we got to the movies it was a whole other story. Browsing the movie selections, we chose another movie – a rated R movie – which was problematic, as Brianne was only fifteen years old.

"Oh, it's okay as long as I'm with someone over twenty-one, and Sophia's twenty-five," she explained. I wasn't too familiar with movie policies so I just assumed that she was right.

We went to the R-rated movie. Afterwards we looked at the clock and realized that we would almost certainly miss curfew. It was already five to ten! None of us had a phone so we borrowed one from the cashier and called for a cab. Then we hung around the theater and waited. The cab company had said it would take between 5 and 30 minutes for a cab to arrive. When 30 minutes had passed and there was still no sign of the cab, we went across the street to the Borders bookstore and hung out there. A kind employee let us use the store phone. We called the cab company again and told them that our cab hadn't come and that we were now at the bookstore. They said someone was on the way. Then we called Renfrew and let them know we were okay.

We waited. And waited. And waited. I did not appear to have much luck with Florida cabs! The store closed and we were still waiting. It was getting late and sketchy characters began appearing on the streets.

"Hey, I was noticing you girls and I decided you were going to talk to us," said a teenaged guy in punk clothing who was smoking from every orifice. The others in his group were silent.

"So?" he continued, "what are your names?"

"Stacy," said Sophia, thinking quickly.

"Amanda," I said, following.

"Holly," said Brianne.

We were clearly not interested but the guy didn't seem to notice or care. *Where was our cab?*

We waited and waited and then decided the cab wasn't coming and we would need to call again. We walked to a nearby drugstore and the cashier let us use the store phone. We called the cab. We also called Renfrew again to let them know we were safe.

After a couple of hours, and several phone calls, the drugstore cashier was getting sick of us.

"I can't keep letting you use the phone," he said, "I'll get in trouble."

We went back outside and sat on the curb, waiting. It was about 12:45 am when the employee from Borders came by and looked at us puzzled.

"Your cab still hasn't come?" he asked. We shook our heads. We told him we didn't think it was coming.

"I can give you a lift," he offered, taking pity on us.

At first I didn't think it was a good idea. But then I re-membered the creepy characters on the street and decided

I needed to get out of there. We briefly discussed it and it seemed like a good idea at the time.

"I think we should do it," I told my friends, "we can't stay out here all night."

We waited for him while he shopped at the drugstore and when he came out we followed him to his car.

"I'll give you a ride," he said, "but you can't kill me or anything." We laughed. I felt more comfortable once he expressed concern about giving strangers a ride home. If *he* was worried, I figured, he couldn't be planning to hurt us. Or could he...?

I was mildly nervous as we got into the car and took off. But he drove us back to Renfrew safely and let us out. We thanked him and said goodnight. In a way I felt exhilarated, like we'd just done something risky and kind of stupid. Which we had. But it felt oddly liberating. We walked toward the residential building talking and laughing. A security guard approached us, radioing that we were back.

"I'm glad you're having such a good time," he said sarcastically. "You had everyone worried sick!" Uh oh...

We went inside to the team center where we were greeted by the nursing staff. It was almost 1:00 am. The nurses gave me my medicine and then sent us off to bed. I was a little concerned about what might happen the next morning, but at that moment I was just so glad to be back at Renfrew, safe and secure. I was also exhausted. I went to bed and slept until morning, trying not to think about all I had to do the next day or about what the consequences of our pass-gone-wrong might be.

The next morning I woke up and tried to focus on the present moment. As it was my last full day at Renfrew, I had a lot to accomplish. I had a family therapy session with Brenda at 8:30 am. I had an individual therapy session later in the day. I had to meet with the financial office, pack my things, meet with various staff members, finalize my aftercare plans, complete the discharge survey, run inspiration celebration, have MST, tell my story to the other women at Renfrew, and of course have people sign my message book and take lots of pictures!

It would be a full day. Honestly I was more excited than overwhelmed. Then I remembered the night before and my stomach fluttered. I tried to relax. *Just go downstairs for vitals*, I told myself. *Take this day one step at a time.*

I put on my gown and went downstairs. When it was my turn for vitals I entered the room and got on the scale.

"I hear you had an interesting night," said the nurse.

"Yeah..." Clearly news of our night out had gotten around fast.

Next I lay down on the table so she could take my blood pressure and pulse. When it was time to take them again in a sitting position another nurse burst in through the door.

"I just yelled at your friends and now I'm going to yell at you!" she exclaimed. "What were you thinking last night?! Going home with a strange man! You could have been killed! And taking an adolescent with you! What were you thinking?!"

At the moment I was thinking that my pulse and blood pressure were going to be sky high and why couldn't she wait another two minutes, but I didn't say that.

"He could have taken you to an empty field! You could have been raped or killed! And you had an adolescent with you!" She went on and on. I listened although I was annoyed that she seemed to care most about Brianne.

After my vitals were finished I left to pick a number and stand in line for my medicine. Outside I saw Sophia. We talked a little bit about the night before. Other girls had already heard about it, because that is the speed of Renfrew gossip. Sophia had gotten criticized most. She'd been told that she was the "adult" since she was the oldest, and that she should have known better. I felt bad for her.

I went to breakfast that morning and tried to avoid the gossip, although I'll admit that it did feel somehow flattering that the others were so interested in our story.

After breakfast I went to meet Brenda for our 8:30 am family session. I waited outside her office for several minutes and when she didn't show up I went down to the team center where I was told she was still in the morning report meeting. I waited outside the team center for her. Finally she came out, looking less than amused.

"I'm late," she said, "because I was busy hearing about your night."

I followed Brenda to her office. I was concerned. How was I going to explain this? Would I get a *chance* to explain? Was I in trouble? What was going to happen to me? Was Brenda disappointed in me? My thoughts were racing as we walked down the hall from the team center to Brenda's office. We went inside her office and Brenda sat down in the chair across from the couch, which is where she sits when we do individual therapy. I was confused. This was supposed to be a family session.

"Sit down," Brenda said.

I sat down. Brenda looked at me expectantly. I looked back at her. I was pretty sure I knew what she wanted, but I did not want to make a mistake.

"So tell me about last night," Brenda started us off. "Hold on, I want to get comfortable..." Brenda curled up in her chair, preparing for the story. It was cute. I told her what had happened the night before. I tried to be as factual as possible.

When I finished Brenda said, "This morning we had a meeting about your pass last night. We were trying to decide what to do about it. I told the other therapists that I wanted to hear it from you first, before we decided on any consequences. I told them that I trust you to tell me the truth. It felt good to be able to say that." It felt good to hear it too. "I'm proud of you."

Brenda did not punish me. She told me that she wanted me to go out on pass again tonight and to make different choices. She said last night was a good learning experience and she reiterated that she trusts me. When we had finished discussing my pass we called my parents and did the family therapy session.

I didn't go to any groups that morning because I was busy doing discharge stuff like meeting with the financial office and packing my things. At one point I was so busy taping together a box that I nearly forgot about inspiration celebration, the patient-run spirituality group comprised of readings, artwork, and other forms of creative expression. I walked as quickly as I could (running is exercise and is not allowed) to the movement room and met up with the staff members in charge of inspiration celebration. I apologized for being late and we went over the last-minute details. At 11:00 am the other girls began piling into the movement room and the program began. The theme was "awareness and self-awareness." I walked up to the podium and addressed the group. I had brought my notes with me, but a last-minute meeting with Elizabeth – a resident with whom I would be leading the 5:00 pm group later that day and telling my story – had convinced me to be brave and speak from the heart.

"When I first came to Renfrew," I began, "I thought I was pretty self-aware. But during my first week here I realized that I was having trouble communicating my needs and getting them met. I resorted to acting out my messages rather than speaking them. Needless to say it didn't help me meet my needs. Renfrew helped me find my voice and in the process of finding my voice I found greater self-awareness. Gaining self-awareness is a process. That's what this week's theme means to me." Then I introduced a series of poems, artwork, and stories.

Since it was my last inspiration celebration I said my goodbye at the end. Again I spoke without notes. It was invigorating to speak without reading, finally not worrying about precision or perfection. I didn't worry about grammar or proper English. I didn't care if what I said was cliché or overused. I would say what was meaningful for me and hope that it held meaning for others. I had grown tremendously.

"Renfrew meant so much to me. I'm going to miss it. For those of you who are just beginning your journeys here, I want you to know that you can accomplish so much here. You can do amazing things. Take advantage of the time, each other, and staff. Continue growing when you leave. I will miss you."

Next I told the group that I had two rocks. I told them I was keeping my "try rock" that I had picked out of the basket during my first healing garden ritual. I had now come to appreciate it on a deeper level. I told the girls that I wanted to keep it to remind me that great things lie in my future but that they require hard work. I wanted to keep it in order to remember that I had come a long way in my journey at Renfrew and it had only happened that way because I had truly tried. I wanted the rock to remind me what I can accomplish when I try.

My other rock was one I had painted with the word "willingness" during a group early on in my stay. At the time I was proud to have been able to fit such a long word on such a small rock using puffy paint. Now I was proud to present the rock to one of my friends at Renfrew who was noticeably struggling in her recovery, but who had recently begun to show willingness to change and open up. She was blossoming before our eyes. I shared this with the roomful of women and gave her the rock. I also told the group that I wanted to leave something behind in the healing garden, as is customary when one leaves Renfrew to symbolize one's recovery.

"I know it's not really a rock," I said, "but it's been *my* 'rock!'" I left my silly putty.

Finally I appointed a new "wand person" for the following week's inspiration celebration. I left the job for a girl who had really begun to come out of her shell and who I thought would benefit from running the group.

After inspiration celebration had ended I went quickly to MST, had individual therapy, met with various staff members about my discharge and finalized my aftercare plans with Claire, my aftercare coordinator.

I was so busy that it wasn't until much later in the day I noticed that Sophia and Brianne were both extremely down. My heart sank. Feeling guilty, I realized immediately that I had been let off much easier than they had been. Sophia wouldn't talk about it right away so I asked Brianne what happened.

It turned out that the blue team had gotten together to discuss our consequences, as two out of the three of us were on the blue team. Sophia and Brianne had both been dropped a level and had to do stage ones the following day. We were all planning to go to the mall that night and our passes had been revoked. I can't say I was heartbroken over the mall passes, but I felt bad that Brianne and Sophia had each lost a level and had to do stage ones, especially when I had gotten off so easy. Although I would no longer be at Renfrew during community the following day, I didn't feel it was fair for them to have to do the stage ones alone. I decided to share in the responsibility and I wrote a letter, showing what I had learned from the experience and my new perspective on the night's events, to be read during the next day's community group.

In the letter I explained what had happened and what a better course of action might have looked like. I apologized for worrying the community. I wrote that safety cannot be taken lightly and that I will make better choices. I photo-copied the letter and gave it to Sophia to read aloud in community the following day.

After I spoke with Brianne about the consequences of our night, I met with Hannah, the blue team leader. I apologized for showing poor judgment and I shared with her what I had learned from the incident. She thanked me for coming by.

After I did all I could to deal with the previous night's fiasco, I got back to my busy last day at Renfrew. I finished packing, painted my name on the wall in the art room – it's a giant autograph wall! – and finished my discharge "to do" list. Finally, all that was left was telling my story to the other women at Renfrew.

11

Week Eleven: Empower Yourself

You can be anything you choose. Your life can be anything you choose. You can be your greatest opponent or your greatest supporter. Only you can decide.

How to

Identify your choices and know what is in your control. Take charge of your life. Employ your skills to help you achieve your dreams. Believe in your own ability to change and grow and live the way you choose. Follow your dreams and live your one life with passion.

When to use this skill

Always.

*a*t 5:00 pm I entered the community room. Although I had been in this room countless times before and although it looked the same, it had a completely different feel this afternoon. Two chairs were set up in the front of the room – one for Elizabeth and one for me. I sat down and the group began. Elizabeth started us off by telling her story. When she had finished it was my turn. I looked around at the group. A roomful of women's faces stared back at me expectantly. I had sat in this room amongst them so many times over the past three months, gleaning insight and inspiration from the various counselors and group leaders, therapists and former residents. It was both mind-boggling and exhilarating to now be the one at the front of the room, telling my story, having others listen and learn from *me*. There was so much to say, so much to express, and not very much time. I hoped I would say the right things. I hoped that I could in some small way, in a brief amount of time, show through my experience that recovery is possible. I hoped I could inspire the other girls and women to work hard, to give them a glimpse of what recovery can mean. I took a deep breath and began my story.

I told them how my eating disorder had begun, how it had escalated over the years and how I had relapsed in Israel at age nineteen. I detailed my denial and rationalization. I described my hitting rock bottom. I explained what went wrong in my previous treatment and how I had ended up at Renfrew. I told the group about my first week in treatment at Renfrew. I was brutally honest in telling what a disaster I had been – how I'd thrown temper tantrums and attempted to run away. I explained my process of recovery – the roles proper nutrition, medication, and therapy had played in my recovery and how certain coping tools, such as mindfulness and using my voice, had helped me progress. I shared my journey through the level system and I read aloud the letter I had written from my body to myself, explaining the significance it held.

Everyone listened attentively as I told my story. I could tell they were truly paying attention. I ended by discussing my current situation – my plans and goals for the future, my fears concerning the transition home. I told everyone that sometimes it feels as though to recover one must never have any fears or doubts at all. I told them that it's not true. I shared with them my own fears – how I still avoided certain foods when I didn't push myself and how I still had body image issues. I told them that it's okay to be scared. It's okay to be imperfect – we all are. I elucidated on my newfound flexibility – it's okay to have plans and goals, but I now know not to lock myself into a set course of action.

Change can be scary and uncomfortable but it's the only way to truly live. I used to think that if I pushed hard enough I could force life to be what I wanted, but now I know that it isn't true. Change gives life vitality and flavor. The flexibility to welcome these changes allows life to be so much richer.

Recovery isn't just about regaining physical, mental, and emotional health. It is about wellness and growth and the discovery of self. It is about living a balanced, meaningful, and fulfilling life. It is the beginning of a journey that lasts a lifetime.

I ended my story and the women applauded. During the question and answer session, one girl who had been at Renfrew longer than I had raised her hand.

"When you first arrived at Renfrew," she said, "I had never seen anyone I thought was so far gone. You've come a long way." There was a lot of nodding from the others who had been there a while.

I got really positive feedback. After the group ended a girl came up to me and told me that I was an inspiration to her. She said that my story had encouraged her and made her feel that she had what it takes to recover. It was such a touching moment.

Throughout the evening women continued to come up to me and thank me for telling my story, to sign my message book, and to say that they would miss me.

The following morning I ate breakfast, gathered my things, and said goodbye to Renfrew. I had come a long way in my eleven weeks there. I could not claim to be fully recovered, but I had begun the lifelong process of recovery. I no longer acted on my urges to restrict my food intake. For the most part I had ceased to compare myself to other eating disorder patients. I had begun taking personal responsibility for my actions – even when I did not *have* to do so. Instead of constantly obsessing over food and body image, I now contemplated what I hoped to accomplish with my life.

Where I once depended on others to meet my emotional needs and take care of me, I could now self-soothe and take care of myself. I still feared the future, but I was learning to accept those fears and live fully. In part, my transition to recovery had been a transition from childhood to adulthood.

I found my voice at Renfrew. I learned to communicate in productive and interpersonally effective ways. I learned to be more flexible and open to life's many changes and developments. I gave up my old, negative coping skills and gained new, positive coping skills. I began the long process of finding myself. I gained the strength and courage to be who I truly am. I found self-acceptance and personal responsibility. I developed greater self-awareness and integrity.

I never achieved perfection.

But as I reflected on the journey I had taken here, I realized that there is no such thing as perfection. There is no such thing as the perfect recovery. Mine certainly wasn't perfect. I had taken a few steps forward and a few steps back. I made progress but not without slips – sometimes significant slips. I had taken advantage of countless opportunities, but had, no doubt, missed countless others. But at Renfrew I learned to do "the next right thing," – that "today is the first day of the rest of my life" – and the possibilities are endless.

It's like Jackie says: don't waste your life on an eating disorder – or anything counterproductive. Follow your dreams and achieve your goals. Live well. Because you only get one life.

One life.

Useful Contacts

The author can be contacted at nfeigenbaum@gmail.com.

The contact details of the treatment centers discussed in this book are listed below:

The Renfrew Centers
Telephone: 1-800-RENFREW
Website: www.renfrewcenter.com
The centers provide a comprehensive range of services in 8 states: Pennsylvania, Florida, New Jersey, New York, Connecticut, North Carolina, Tennessee and Texas.

The Cleveland Center for Eating Disorders (CCED)
Telephone: 216-765-0500
Website: www.edcleveland.com
The center is committed to providing effective treatment for children, adolescents and adults suffering from an eating disorder.

Index